CW00369916

Rough Diamonds & Real Gems

R. M. Winn was a rural valuer, cow cocky and tried his hand at about fifty other jobs before becoming a full-time writer. He changed vocations midstream when a brain tumour laid him low for a few years. He has seven other books to his credit, the I Kid You Not trilogy, *High Tides & Hard Rides*, *When a Tree Falls*, *Behind the Bike Shed* and *A Kick to the Head*, which continues to earn praise as an inspirational book in Australia.

Rhylle lives at Dayboro (which doesn't show up on any map) in Queensland with his long-suffering wife, Karyn, who has empty-nest syndrome – a condition that can only be treated by half a dozen grandchildren.

Rhylle suspects he might be related to Henry Lawson because Henry's granny, Harriet Winn, and Rhylle's great-great grandfather, James Winn, both arrived in Mudgee in the 1840s, but he doesn't really want to find out because Henry was a real pisspot.

Rhylle's other books are all available on back list directly from the author: rhylleandk@optusnet.com.au.

R.M. WINN

Rough Diamonds & Real Gems

VIKING
an imprint of
PENGUIN BOOKS

VIKING

Published by the Penguin Group
Penguin Group (Australia)
250 Camberwell Road, Camberwell, Victoria 3124, Australia
(a division of Pearson Australia Group Pty Ltd)
Penguin Group (USA) Inc.
375 Hudson Street, New York, New York 10014, USA
Penguin Group (Canada)
90 Eglinton Avenue East, Suite 700, Toronto, Canada ON M4P 2Y3
(a division of Pearson Penguin Canada Inc.)
Penguin Books Ltd
80 Strand, London WC2R 0RL England
Penguin Ireland
25 St Stephen's Green, Dublin 2, Ireland
(a division of Penguin Books Ltd)
Penguin Books India Pvt Ltd
11 Community Centre, Panchsheel Park, New Delhi – 110 017, India
Penguin Group (NZ)
67 Apollo Drive, Rosedale, North Shore 0632, New Zealand
(a division of Pearson New Zealand Ltd)
Penguin Books (South Africa) (Pty) Ltd
24 Sturdee Avenue, Rosebank, Johannesburg 2196, South Africa

Penguin Books Ltd, Registered Offices: 80 Strand, London, WC2R 0RL, England

First published by Penguin Group (Australia), 2007

1 3 5 7 9 10 8 6 4 2

Copyright © Rhylle Winn 2007

The moral right of the author has been asserted

All rights reserved. Without limiting the rights under copyright reserved above,
no part of this publication may be reproduced, stored in or introduced into a retrieval
system, or transmitted, in any form or by any means (electronic, mechanical, photocopying,
recording or otherwise), without the prior written permission of both the copyright owner
and the above publisher of this book.

Text and cover design by Debra Billson © Penguin Group (Australia)
Cover photograph by Oliver Strewe/Lonely Planet Images
Author photograph by Chris Higgins
Typeset in 12/18 pt Fairfield LH Light by Post Pre-press Group, Brisbane, Queensland
Printed and bound in Australia by McPherson's Printing Group, Maryborough, Victoria

National Library of Australia
Cataloguing-in-Publication data:

Winn, Rhylle, 1949–.
Rough diamonds and real gems.
ISBN 978 0 143 00647 3.
1. Australians – Biography. I. Title.

920.094

penguin.com.au

In memory of Colin Thiele, AC

RHYLLE WINN
An ordinary bloke

——•◆•——

I'm not an extraordinary bloke. I'm just an ordinary one. Maybe what has happened to me over the years is extraordinary, but I've had no control over any of it. It's just nature at work. Right place at the right time – wrong place at the wrong time, or any combination. Lots of the people who have shaped my life, well, to me, they're the extraordinary ones.

I used to tell stories; bullshit most of it – so they said – but good fun.

Now I write stories; no bullshit any more – much – and they say it's different, keep going.

I used to drive cattle trucks; rough hard dirty work, and I loved it. Now they have taken my heavy transport licence off me.

I used to own a 20 000-acre cattle property and several teams of working dogs – now I own one lazy canine remnant and a measly 3 acres.

I used to imbibe – mostly too much – and now I'm nearly tee-total. Now *that's* extraordinary.

Something changed me. Something drastic.

I was a bit different right from day one. No, it wasn't my body or brain that was different, it was how I was branded – no input from me at all.

If I start right at the beginning, within a couple of hours of my birth, you'll understand. Laugh if you want. I'm nearly used to it now. It's only taken fifty years. You know that song of Johnny Cash's 'A Boy Named Sue' (how do you do)? Well Sue and I have something in common. His father named him Sue – to make him tough. My mother named me Rhylle – to square off with the big boss upstairs because she wanted a girl. She'd show him. She'd give me a girl's name. So that's how it happened and I guess I'm stuck with it.

Gatherings where they already have a name tag printed out for you and pin it to your pocket as you enter the room are the worst. I usually turn mine over and pretend to be unaware of the fact.

A well-groomed young lady across the room makes eye contact. She comes over; attractive she is and looks like she'd hold her own anywhere.

'Hello,' she says, turning my name tag over. 'Well isn't that a pretty name, where'd your mum find that one? I went to school with a girl named "Rill". We used to call her "Rill the dill",' and she covers her mouth pretending to suppress her giggle.

Or, a bloke on the other side of the room glances my way. He probably feels sorry for me standing there all alone like a country dunny, and he wanders over to have a talk. As he gets closer he focuses on my name tag. I bet he's thinking, *What the hell's his name? Shit! How do I pronounce that? Bloody multiculturalism.* So he simply nods to me and veers off to talk to Gloria behind the bar instead, as if that had been his intention all along.

It's lonely being a Sue, I can tell you.

So I take the bloody tag off and drop it into the pot plant.

But all is not lost. A voice behind me says, 'Ah, g'day mate, enjoying the program? Not bad is it?'

See? Straight away, a new friend. He probably thinks I'm the cleaner because I don't have a name tag, and everybody is always pleasant to the cleaner.

Growing up, I know I was a bastard of a kid. My parents nicknamed me 'Bulldozer': I liked that a lot better than Rhylle. They said I was a good kid, really, but required a fair bit of direction. Parents in the '50s still clung to the idea that wayward kids needed a regular clip in the lug, and teachers thought a good caning would help. It never dawned on them that I wasn't the slow learner; *they* were.

A lot of my time was spent alone, by choice. I had a good dog, a good horse, a good .22 rifle and an adventurous spirit. Dressed like Davy Crockett I roamed our 500 acres and thousands of acres that belonged to our neighbours. I dreamed of owning a big cattle property one day.

At the other end of the farm, near our sawmill, were four families of uncles and aunts and their ten children, in addition to other itinerant families of sharefarmers and millworkers. No wonder a kid had to get away on his own, but really, the extended family was wonderful.

Primary school was an interlude, boarding school a shock, a total of six soul-destroying years in the public service boring beyond belief. Christ, is this all that life offers? So I threw it all away and went exploring.

Someone said to Dad once, 'Lived all your life in this district, Richie?' To which he replied, 'Not yet.'

'Finished buggering around and wasting your life Rhylle?'

'Not yet.'

Hereditary? Must be.

My father, Richie (nicknamed McGinty), was my mate and the first extraordinary character to enter my life. He's gone now. He conked out just a few years ago. He was eighty-seven.

'Come on son, let's hop into it.'

I hated bloody fencing. Mechanical post-hole borers were everywhere, but we still did it all by hand with the bar and shovel.

'By the time you go and borrow a bloody borer we can have half of them done.'

'What about the other half, Dad?'

'Well by the time you take it back we'll have them done too. Otherwise you'll spend most of the day running backwards and forwards instead of working.'

'Yeah but . . . Well why don't we buy one?'

'Wouldn't have much use for one, would we? Only do a bit of fencing now and again.'

I thought, *bullshit*, but dared not utter it. I knew I couldn't win.

'Dad, I want to go home.'

'We'll just do a few more. Then we will.'

'How many more?'

'Just a few. Every one we do is one less we have to do.'

Whenever I thought he wasn't watching I'd fill the holes in quickly without ramming them much.

'Ram it properly son. Be a bugger if you had to do it again.'

It was always dark when we got home. Dad loved work, physical work. He was fit and tough his whole life. I thought all dads were like that.

Later, as a school project, I became interested in our family history.

'Dad, when you used to drive bullocks, how many did you have in a team?'

'Fourteen or sixteen. Many more and they were too hard to handle in steep or rough country. With longer logs, anything over about fifteen or sixteen foot was too long for big teams to pull around corners. They got pulled over the side.'

'What, the bullocks?' I was aghast at the thought.

'No, the bloody logs,' he laughed, then went on, 'but there was one time when my grandfather's team did go over the side of a bridge, or some of them did. Your great grandfather – Old Dick everybody called him. It was his good team.'

I was all ears.

'He was pulling a wagon loaded with bridge girders and when the team stepped onto the new bridge – it didn't have any side logs, that's what his wagon was loaded with – one of his leaders didn't want to go on and pushed his mate sideways, off the edge.'

'Geez! What happened then?'

'It wasn't too bad because they weren't very far onto the bridge. Only about six of the twenty-two went over. One leader was killed, not the one that caused the trouble either. The others were only knocked about a bit. They were working again the next week with a new leader.'

Bullockies and their teams were commonplace in Australia's early days but not many teams were still being worked after World War II. Dad's was. He was the last commercial bullocky in our district.

'What happened when all your team died, Dad? There's a bit about it in this old paper I found on top of your cupboard.'

'What bloody cupboard? You keep out of there or I'll tan your hide! Here, show me. Christ I haven't seen that for thirty years. What else was up there?'

'Only an old book about cows' diseases and a couple of empty envelopes.'

'Yeah, fourteen were dead within two days and the other two never worked again,' he said as he read the faded newspaper clipping.

He went quiet, a faraway look in his eyes.

I knew not to say any more. *He'll tell me later*, I thought.

Dad was only fourteen when he took charge of his own team. He'd had the choice of two. Old Dick was his mentor, driving another team alongside for the first few months. Then McGinty was on his own.

'That's not so young, son. Old Dick took charge of a team when he was ten. He drove it through the night with his badly crushed father on top of the wagon half-loaded with logs. That's true my boy, and I've kept the newspaper cutting about it. They told the whole story in his obituary. I'll show you.'

And so he did. I've got it now. I treasure it.

'You know when your team died, Dad, what happened?' He hadn't mentioned it again and I still didn't have an answer.

'Red lantana killed them, son. They ate it while I was spelling them at lunchtime and after I took their nosebags off. I had pulled in close to the side of the track and they could reach the lantana with their long tongues. It was a dry time and they were back in condition a bit. The green pick enticed them. Normally they wouldn't eat it. I should have noticed. It was my fault.'

His momentary silence betrayed the hurt, still.

He went on. 'It would be the same as losing a big truck today. That was how I made my living. It took a long while getting over that, my boy.'

'What did you do?'

'I always had another young team coming on so I put them to work as babies. Ended up the best little outfit in the district – go anywhere and keep going they would. One was a little Jersey for God's sake. I only put him in to even up the pairs. He was so little. I put him in the body of the team to start to teach him to pull, and you know what? He was eventually the best leader I ever had. Little hard black feet he had, like all Jerseys. Never ever got footsore. And smart he was, could read the track like you wouldn't believe.'

'What was his name?'

'"Pilot", the little bloke, and his pair was "Captain".'

'What about the others – their names I mean?'

He nodded slowly.

'I could never forget that last team. What a great bunch of little troopers. That was one of their names, "Trooper". His mate was "Topsy".'

'And the others?'

'Righto. Captain and Pilot, Topsy and Trooper, Major and Bright,

Rover and Speck, Cherry and Knob, Sailor and Rattler, Sunny and Charmer, Tiger and Punch. There you are, how's that for a good memory? That was their order in the team.'

I was enthralled. Dad's life seemed an adventure that belonged to another time. *Dad* belonged to another time. Modern life had passed him by in many ways. Mum always said of his car driving that he learned to drive on bullocks and never improved, even to the extent of saying 'whoa bullocks!' then driving the car through the end of the shed, taking the complete wall with him – like a bullbar, Mum joked. Certainly his speed was similar to that of the bullocks. But he was happy with his lot – always happy, and always working.

My most enduring memory of him, the one that first springs to mind so easily each time I think of him is this one. I was with him when he had to go to the bank to apply for a bridging loan for the very first time in his life – the result of a very unfortunate, and thankfully only temporary, setback. He was sixty-two.

The bank manager, or bank johnny as Dad always called them, was condescending towards the hardened old bushman with the gnarled hands. Dad was nervous and it showed. The manager either didn't recognise my father's nervousness, or chose to do nothing to allay his fears.

When the forms were pushed towards Dad for signature, they had already been signed by the manager, which I thought was most unusual. He must have realised his mistake because he became agitated when Dad took the document, perused it thoroughly and then handed it to me. We could have altered the figures and it would still have had his approval. Now the form was out of his hands. He could hardly jump up and snatch it back.

I looked at the manager's signature: 'J. Wills JP' – then caught his eye and smiled a little. I had some slight knowledge of these matters and he must have realised. The tables were turned. Now he was the edgy one. Dad finished reading, looked him squarely in the eye and with great deliberation reached forward and signed, 'R. R. Winn OC'.

The johnny took a deep breath, of relief I think, then looked down at the signature, looked up at Dad, then down at the signature again. He'd taken Dad for a fool and the bushman had letters after his name.

Outside I said to Dad, 'You never told us you had any formal qualifications.'

'Didn't I?'

'What's it mean?'

'I made that bastard sit up and take notice, don't you reckon?'

'What is it Dad?'

'Oxen Conductor, son, Oxen Conductor,' and he winked at me.

I was twenty and being a trainee rural land valuer with the public service was sheer drudgery. I had to work all day and go to college most nights. I didn't really have my heart in it – I wanted my life to go faster than that – so I chucked it in part way through. There was so much activity going on at home and I was loath to miss out.

My interests lay in the mill and logging outfit. Circular saws singing their dangerous song and sawdust blasting out of the big blower; Aunty Monica whistling to Uncle Jim to come to the phone, the big winch in the mill and the two little winches on the tractors straining to their limits daily; the high-revving machinery dying down at half-past four – music to our ears. It was so regular, so familiar, so mundane – and I loved it.

I wanted to operate the logging unit's two dozers – one with a blade and one without. I wanted to drive the big V8 Ford pulling the jinker. I wanted to go back to the heart of our family – and I did.

I went bush and worked with Uncle Ben. He was the bush manager and I was keen to learn the game. Dad was thrilled that I had the opportunity.

'Ben, you'll lose half your tools through this hole in the floor.'

We were on our way to work in his old ute.

'Might. Haven't yet.'

'How'd it get there?' The rest of the old girl was sound. This wasn't a rust hole.

'I bashed it through with the cold chisel.'

'Why?'

'The reason is closely associated with this window.'

I looked quizzically at him. There was no glass in it.

'I can't do much to stop the rain coming in through here, but the least I can do is let it out after it has,' he laughed.

'Oh, okay . . .' I should have guessed. A typical Ben solution to a minor annoyance.

Ben was the larrikin of the family – the larrikin with the soft heart and mountains of ability. He taught me so much about everything: the job, mechanics, building houses, how to laugh, and the grog – and all of that was just the beginning. He was an extraordinary bloke.

Each morning we'd leave the sawmill early, the log truck following on behind, and weave our way through the valleys. Patient dairy cattle beside milking sheds breathed winter steam or lolled summer tongues, while blasts of frosty air or hot wind blew onto Ben's face, or up my pants leg through the jagged hole in the floor pan. Stifling mornings became cooler as we rose up into the mountains. Similarly, lowland briskness dissipated somewhat at increasing altitude. But the temperature made no difference to the crystal symphony of countless bell birds. This was our workplace.

Alighting from the ute at a small clearing, we'd board the clanking monster in the form of a Caterpillar dozer and disappear down the steep slopes into the depths of the scrub. It was a trial for the truck and jinker to descend such extreme grades, so a heavy chain linked the back of the truck to the blade of the tractor and in effect the dozer lowered the truck to the bottom.

Truck loaded, the reverse applied. It didn't have either the power or the traction to ascend under its own steam so the dozer went in front and towed it out.

Smoko at the top. Most mornings, a 3-metre carpet python paid us a visit. In due course he became a pet of sorts. It broke Ben's heart to have to kill him one morning after we'd parked on him as we'd arrived. The stricken reptile was not discovered till smoko and nothing could be done to save him.

After smoko, the dozer routinely clanked back down to snig another load and the truck with its load of logs went off to the mill, at that time driven by my seventeen-year-old cousin Barry.

At the outset my job was 'blue tonguing' – the slow-moving

dozer was a stocky short-tailed lizard and the grey wire rope running off the winch spool his tongue, flicking out regularly to secure his meal of logs. It was bloody hard work. Easy enough to pull the rope down the near-vertical cliffs but far too dangerous to ride the logs back up. I'd never been so fit.

On the way home one afternoon I said to Ben, who I think was contemplating a few cold beers at the time, 'Are we going to fix that oil leak in the diff?'

He'd discovered it after he'd despatched the snake.

'Arr, won't bother yet.'

'Why not? If it runs out of oil it'll be buggered.'

He shook his head, 'While there's some leaking out we know there's still some in there.'

'Yeah, plenty till it runs out, eh? Granny was Irish, wasn't she?'

'Your granny was Scottish. My granny was Irish.'

For a moment I thought I was adopted.

'That might explain a few things. All tight with the purse strings and a bit, what'll we say, a bit lateral in our thinking.'

'What?'

'You know, see things a bit different.'

'A lot different. I like the Irish. They're all bloody good workers. Like Reg.'

Stocky little Reg was the benchman in the mill, and he could work, day in, day out, and never miss a beat.

After a while he spoke again, 'Yeah I suppose a bloke should tidy that diff up a bit. Come back Saturday and we'll give her a going over. She's due for a bit of a service.'

'Okay.'

'I'll pull the front plate off it and put a bit of gorilla snot around the flange and tighten it back up. That'll fix it. This old tub has done a lot of work.'

I nodded, thinking, *Ben and his bloody 'gorilla snot'*. He seals up everything with gorilla snot. And he calls degreaser 'possum piss' and grease 'slippery dick'. We'd grown up with his metaphors and they were familiar language to us. With Ben no aspect of life was ever taken too seriously. It was a joy to work with him.

Midmorning one day some months later, I received an urgent phone call from home. I wasn't working with Ben at the time. Heeding family advice I'd gone back to finish my valuation course in the city. I'd have to do it, like it or not. The writing was on the wall. The mill was to be resumed by the government for a dam. There was to be no future for us in the timber industry.

'Go quickly to Royal Brisbane Hospital. There's been an accident up the bush. Ben might not make it.'

Panic surged through me. Arriving at the hospital I was met by some of the family. My father and uncles looked strangely out of place in the sterile atmosphere of the hospital ward.

'What happened? Is he going to be okay?' I asked breathlessly, my voice edged with fear.

'A big springy ironbark sapling rode up over the blade as he was pushing in a new road. It was loaded between two others and as it cleared the blade it whipped back and hit Ben in the chest. It'll be touch and go, they reckon.'

Jim's voice trailed off as he stood staring through the ward window at the street below.

Ben looked ghastly. It was more go than touch, I thought.

'After all these years, no canopy or anything, never a problem,' I said to no one in particular.

He lay there deathly pale, unmoving. I searched his face for a flicker of recognition but there was none. I said my goodbye to Ben, for ever, I thought, and walked out in tears. He lingered on for a few days, then rallied. How, nobody knew.

He was badly damaged, but by the grace of some higher being he survived.

'Some higher being be buggered. I wanted to get out and have a few beers and a Rothmans or two.'

Why weren't we surprised? His extreme fitness had held him in good stead, they said, and by degrees he recovered.

He brushed aside any suggestion of toughness, 'No I just made a new appointment with the devil. He was too busy just then. Too many other bastards to process.'

To celebrate Ben's recovery I went and got married. Or maybe I should word that differently. During Ben's recovery I asked Karyn, my high school sweetheart, to marry me – a pretty little school-teacher with a beautiful nature and a silken voice. I married a kid when I was just a kid myself. Twenty and twenty-one we were. Being a romantic she thought she was marrying Rhett Butler, the lead character in *Gone with the Wind*. It must have been a shock for her, poor kid, when she realised I was his long-lost third cousin *Harry* Butler, the knockabout Aussie naturalist.

Within a short space of time we had two little ones to care for. What a joy. But being a valuer, albeit now a qualified one, was not for me. My heart was simply not in it, so I tossed it in a second time and we took off – in a short-wheelbase Landcruiser – with kids Ben (three) and Kylie (eighteen months) – and a tent – to circumcise Australia.

'That's ridiculous,' Karyn said, when I told her my circumcise joke. 'You're getting worse every day.'

'Think about it. If we cut Tasmania off the trip . . .'

She shook her head, laughing.

We had grand plans but money was the problem – we ran out. We'd made it to Cairns and as luck would have it I landed a job with a gang harvesting sugar cane – at first bin hauling beside the harvester then later cutting plant cane by hand. A good job, good pay, good people. Savino Benedetti was the boss. He and his family took us in and showered us with hospitality. They showed us a different way of life.

I remember soot-blackened faces late in the hotel and cinder-blackened washing forgotten on the clothesline – how the women complained on both counts and how the men took no notice. I can see and hear them now. Savino and Mario with their Italian accents, Darum and Tara the Indians, José and Lupi Spanish to the core. The Kiwi was the only one I could understand completely, but he knew as much about the lingo as I did, and that didn't help. After a while I was speaking broken English. So was he.

Start-up time in the early mornings was the most difficult. Garbled orders in a string of languages, accompanied by arms waving every which way, saw everybody head off in different directions – except Kiwi and me. We would look at each other, shrug and wait. They'd come back. They always did.

'Shit. Sorry fellas. I forgot again you don speak the lingo. You come with me. You catch up with Mario and Darum.'

Off we'd roar on the haul-out tractors.

'We'll burn again tonight,' Savino announced at lunchtime, 'pick you up at eight o'clock.'

Because Karyn and I were staying in the barracks on the property while the others travelled to work each day it made sense for me to accompany Savino.

'Now look out for taipans. If we go quick around the edge with the drip torches, we maybe cook the lot – eh.'

'Look out for taipans! For Christ's sake, Savino, it's pitch black.'

'Yeah we go fast then, eh. Probably see a bit when she goes up.'

'And that makes it better? Shit, how many men get bitten?'

'Only a few. You'll be right.'

'Only a few – how often? Only a few each season?'

'No, none last year.'

I wondered, did that mean there were a few the year before? I had snake phobia for hours. But we burnt three or four acres every night and I soon became quite blasé about the taipans and other critters that might have lurked there. I didn't get bitten but I got the fright of my life when a rat ran right up my pants' leg. Not liking his surrounds, or something, he quickly did an about turn and retreated, but not before my heart nearly knocked the pocket off my shirt.

I took to all aspects of the work like a dung beetle to a cow-pat and soon got the hang of loading the 5-ton bins on the move beside the harvester. It entailed constantly repositioning the tractor under the elevator chute of the harvester and shaking down the chopped billets of cane with intermittent jerks on the clutch. When I could fill a bin and pyramid the top without spilling a stick I had completed my apprenticeship and was treated as an equal by the other workmen. In fact Savino was proud of the new bin hauler, he said. He told everyone, usually after six or seven pots of North Queensland lager, that he'd taught me well.

I got the impression that if you could work as well as an Italian you were as good as one. In fact, with my complexion I looked like one. A real bonus.

The Commercial Hotel in Gordonvale often beckoned. How could we resist after boiling in our skins all day every day? No air-cabs on the tractors in those days. The pub was the hub of Italian commerce and as Savino's guest I mostly drank there. At the beginning I felt out of place. Not for long.

'Hey youse blokes. My mate here don speak the lingo. Only Aussie when he's here, okay?' They all nodded.

The barman, Aldo, a second-generation Aussie himself, called me over later that first evening when things had quietened down a little.

'I thought you *paisan*, countryman, eh. You looka like one of us. Keepa your fuckin' mouth shut and nobody ever know you're not, eh,' he said genially.

I knew by then that most often, true to the North Queensland peculiarity, 'eh' was really only the bottom half of Aldo's question mark and didn't need an answer. When he asked a real question he added the second 'eh' with a rising inflexion, equivalent to scribing the crook above the full stop.

'Where you come from then eh – *eh?*'

'Ireland, Cornwall and Scotland. That's where the ancestors came from.'

'Huh, fuckin' Pom eh. But you're all right – not like most of those fuckin' lazy union bastards eh. Savvy tells me you can work. You're okay then. He knows eh.'

I thought, *thank you Aldo, I'm bloody well pleased about that.*

I worked the full season of seven months, cutting out just after New Year. After being fired up for so long, totally focused, long hours in sweltering conditions, the season's end hit hard. It was such an anti-climax, especially for Savino who looked like he'd run over Brutus, the big useless mutt that he loved. But the district was abuzz. The itinerants among the cane workers packed up in a frenzy. They wanted to be first off the blocks in the race to Victoria, and other parts south, to snaffle the best fruit-picking jobs. The Bruce Highway wasn't the safest place to be as the southern exodus began.

Cashed up, we prepared to fulfil our original intention, which had been to drive anticlockwise around the coastline. That was the detailed itinerary – a bit open-ended, you could say. Even now it wasn't to be. The weather, the wet they call it, released the season's quota in a week, then just for good measure developed into a cyclone, and released the same again, plus a bit more. Anticlockwise be buggered, we bolted south down the coast, tailing the last of the fruit pickers, and being shadowed every inch of the way by wild, wild weather.

Not to be thwarted we departed once more from Brisbane, continuing south in a clockwise direction – with a 12-gauge shotgun strapped across the dashboard and adventure in our hearts.

That single-shot Winchester was our security (there were no mobile or satellite phones then). It was to play a bit part in the coming months, though perhaps more than a bit part in the minds of a couple of unfortunates. The Nullarbor Plain in those days was still mostly a dirt track – a long dreary drive, and very slow. But there was no hurry. We had forever, or when Ben started school, whichever came first.

One scorching midday as we bumped over the corrugated patches and swerved through the sand drifts, we spied a stationary car on the road up ahead. Unusual, I thought, particularly as we approached and focused on two men in trousers, white shirts and ties no less. They stood waving us down. I was wary.

I said to Karyn, 'I'll drive past them slowly and we'll get a look at them and see what they want. Then we'll pull up a bit further along.'

'Be careful, remember we've got the kids. Maybe we shouldn't stop at all.'

They looked for all the world like Don Corleone and a swarthy bodyguard. As we idled past, one of them held up a radiator hose. It was either a genuine distress signal or a good decoy, but I couldn't just drive on. We stopped.

I unstrapped the shotgun and left it loose on the seat, telling Karyn to scare them with it if necessary. Then I got out and walked back. As usual I was relying on her to stay calm and in charge. A lot of women might have quaked at such a request.

As I approached, my concern dissipated – a trail of water told the story. The stranded travellers had obviously blown a radiator hose, and almost certainly the one that had been held aloft as we'd passed. As I opened my mouth to speak, Ben, now nearly four, leaned out of the driver's window of the cruiser and yelled back to me at the top of his lungs, 'Do you want the gun yet, Dad?'

The looks of sheer terror on the faces of the two business types is indelibly etched in my mind. It was one of those priceless moments. They took some reassuring. To allay their fears I called out to Karyn to bring the water bag, to at least partly fill their radiator. They could see I wasn't armed and had a good chance to ascertain that she wasn't either. They'd had a new radiator hose with them and had fitted it but carried no spare water – a dangerous oversight in the most remote and arid place in the country.

They relaxed somewhat after their radiator was fully operational again. Their tense expressions softened and we all laughed about our former fears – strained laughs perhaps. You don't have to love your neighbour, but you can do him a good turn.

'Hope they don't miss the funeral, or more importantly the wake,' I said to Karyn as they took off at pace in front of us.

'Look on the bright side. It's probably the groom and best man running a bit late for the wedding,' she replied.

We were on the road for a full year. Life was so good. We thought those days would never end – that they'd never change. No, that's not really right. You don't think about it at the time. It's only later when they *have* ended that you do.

My dream of owning a big cattle property still beckoned, and the idea of starting with a little one appealed. Karyn backed me up and we followed that dream. Our third child Dan was born just after we took possession of a 100-acre former dairy farm at Dayboro, forty kilometres northwest of Brisbane.

What a ride that would be! Karyn went along with all my hare-brained moneymaking schemes. She believed in me and I don't know how or why. (I'm not game to bring up the subject now. But we laugh a lot.)

Money was scarce. In dollar terms we were poor, but life was so rich. Subsistence farming by necessity is one thing – by choice another. We chose the challenge and it was fun. It was also bloody hard work.

Home-grown beef, pork, poultry, milk, eggs, fruit and vegetables; homemade butter, biscuits and bread. We grew small crops for sale, sold sides of beef and cured hams to neighbours. We made do very well with very little.

The TV broke down, and stayed that way for three years. But boy, could the kids play monopoly, cards and scrabble. Ben told his little schoolmate, 'We haven't got any money, but my dad can make anything and fix everything.'

I suppose I still can.

Hired labour for bigger projects was not a consideration. Karyn was the long-suffering offsider. She picked watermelons, drove the tractor, helped with fencing and loaded hay. One stormy evening just after dark we discovered a heavily pregnant sow had escaped from her pen. There was no mistake about it – she was standing at the back steps with her snout in the scraps bin. It was imperative that we return her to her pen as she was due to farrow, probably that night. It wasn't hard to entice her back to her sty with the balance of the scraps, but having just achieved that, and pushing her back through her escape hole, we were startled by a blinding flash of lightning that blew a nearby transformer to a thousand bits and blacked the place out.

'Jesus Christ! Karyn, you hold this sheet of iron over the hole while I go and get a torch.' I thought this seemed a reasonable request even though it was now pitch black.

'Don't leave me here! Don't leave me in the dark. What if she tries to escape again?'

'You'll be right. I'll only be a minute. Just hold it in place.'

It's a fact that if a pig can get its snout through a hole then the rest of it will shortly follow. It wasn't long before the pig pushed past the sheet of iron despite Karyn's best efforts. On my way back, tripping and slipping through blinding rain, another flash of lightning revealed a scene almost like a kid's cartoon.

The pig had squeezed between Karyn's legs, picking her up on the way, and was careering across the newly ploughed cultivation with Karyn riding her, backwards.

My poor little wife fell off into the mud and lay there sobbing. I thought she was hurt and my heart went out to her. She wasn't, but she took some consoling. It was morning before I was game to laugh and much later before she did. Rhett Butler indeed!

In any case the pig returned to her pen of her own accord. She'd probably always intended to. She had eleven healthy babies by morning.

We spent years on that little farm. It was a perfect place to rear kids and only the first few years were lean. Karyn returned to schoolteaching and I practised as a rural valuer (in due course becoming the only valuer in the shire) and spent many hours as an expert witness in every type of court in Australia – from the Supreme Court down. I was eventually thankful that the family had persuaded me to complete my course, but I still didn't like it any more than when I'd started.

My ambition to own my own cattle property became a burning desire, a dream yet to be fulfilled. Daily I scanned the papers for something that might suit. Visions of surveying the Ponderosa from a high vantage point while mounted on a black stallion often filled my mind. Too many Westerns.

I didn't find my dream cattle station but what I did find was a 20 000-acre property for lease on an island just off the coast of Central Queensland. We took it on with a partner. However, our six-year lease was curtailed after three, cutting short what had been shaping up to be the adventure of a lifetime. Still, I'd had a taste of running a property on a larger scale and the call of owning my own cattle property grew stronger each day. I had to follow it.

I was forty-four – healthy, happy and could work like a bullock. Karyn shared my love of life. The family was off our hands, sort of. We had some hard-earned cash in the bank and were once again looking for adventure.

We found it, our personal Ponderosa, in the form of a property named Trinity, an almost intact original selection in the South Burnett region of south-east Queensland. It boasted about 3000 acres, two homes and outbuildings, sheds and a good set of yards. Carrying capacity was 300 beef breeders and 250 acres of dryland cultivation.

Trinity – the union of three, the Father, the Son and the Holy Spirit. How biblical! But perhaps there is no holy connection. Perhaps the name has more to do with the three creeks – Chinkie, Undaban and Trinity – that meet on the boundary. Trinity is situated in the heartland of the quaintly titled and aptly described Bible Belt. It is a well-defined area, and to derogatory politicians, a slightly amusing phenomenon well used at State election time. God-botherers do abound on all sides. It was somewhat incongruous having us join the community. I think at times we may have added another dimension to their lives.

The property was run down and it was a challenge to bring it back to former prosperity. Enthusiasm can do wonders, making hard work a joy and a fulfilment. We had plenty of all three. Trinity saw to that.

It was a dream fulfilled. Then . . .

I don't think I can do this. Get a hold of yourself. Of course you can. The thoughts cartwheeled through my mind. How could it be any worse than being challenged by a brumby stallion or being bailed up behind a gate by a scrubber cow? I knew it had to be done, but I didn't want this. The feelings welled up inside. I knew I was shaking. I wanted to get out of here. I wanted to go back . . .

'Mr Winn, try to calm down. You have to cooperate. There is no alternative. You're no good the way you are. Let us help you.'

I nodded.

I'd started having seizures with increasing regularity, and we had to find out why.

'Lie down here on this trolley. We'll have to put a couple of straps across your body to help hold you still. Are you claustrophobic?'

I submitted and tried to relax. *Am I claustrophobic?* A vision of crawling through a concrete drainpipe under our road to repair a polythene water line that runs through it comes to mind. The pipe's diameter was barely the width of my shoulders. It was 60 feet long and water trickled under me, soaking the front of my shorts. The water was iridescent green and I was loath to think why. I blocked any light from behind and all I had to work by was the illuminated pinpoint in front. I relied almost entirely on my sense of touch. And the only problem I felt I had was with the swallows' nests almost touching my head and the thought of a shower of lice if I disturbed them.

'No not particularly,' I finally remembered to answer.

'Okay, lie still now.' The hands tending me were strong and practised, the voice businesslike.

One strap across my chin – too tight for comfort – one across my upper body pinning my arms and more further down, I thought. Were there?

'This will take about forty-five minutes. It will be very noisy and you must remain absolutely motionless. There will be a break of a minute or two in the middle. Okay? Can you do this for us?'

I tried to nod, and blinked instead.

'If you absolutely have to stop and have to come out then press this rubber ball. But try not to. This is an expensive procedure and there is a long waiting list to use it. You have jumped the queue because of the seriousness of your case.'

'Bullshit, who said that?'

One nurse looked towards another with raised eyebrows.

'Come on Mr Winn, let's get on with it.'

And so they did. The trolley I'm strapped to runs on rails into a black tunnel. I got three-quarters of the way in and squeezed the ball.

'What is it Mr Winn?'

'It's too tight. I can't fit.'

'Yes you can. We have others a lot bigger than you go through.'

'Just give me thirty seconds and I'll blank out. I can do it. I used to do it as a kid when I had my teeth filled without needles.'

'Yes, okay.'

'I can't feel anything if I concentrate. I can separate my mind from my body. It's like finding another dimension.' I felt suddenly lucid and surprised myself. Surely there can't be too much wrong.

They both nodded, but I could tell they didn't believe me. I collected my thoughts and we tried again.

Nothing registered. Then I woke up and it was very quiet and pitch black. *Where am I? Am I dead?* I nearly panicked, then I remembered.

Halfway through.

I fought to regain control and succeeded. The next thing I knew the trolley was moving again.

'That wasn't too bad, was it?'

'What?' Then I remembered to say, 'No, I don't think so.'

I'd had an MRI scan at Royal Brisbane Hospital. Apparently I was crook. How could that be? I felt like I could spring out of bed and ride 80 kilometres on a good horse. The next minute I could barely keep awake.

I was admitted to Royal Brisbane. I remember counting echoing footsteps fading in the distance then others becoming louder as someone approached. And then they faded too. Voices rose and fell to match. Something rattled past. If it was the tea trolley it should have stopped. It didn't. Alien smells pervaded my senses. It was all different. Momentarily I was all different. Then I was myself again. Confused.

I had the family with me. 'The doctor will come in soon,' I was told, 'with the results of the scan.' We waited, making small talk then retreating into private thoughts.

He entered the ward. The nurse who was taking my blood pressure told me he was the surgeon, a very highly regarded one just home from the States after a stint at the world-class Mayo Clinic.

'What the bloody hell does he want with me? Who said anything about a surgeon? I've watched enough episodes of M*A*S*H to know all about surgeons.'

I looked to Karyn and the family. Did they know more than I did?

He looked just like an ordinary bloke, about the same height and a bit younger than me. He viewed the scan and dropped a bombshell. The only words I heard were, 'Brain tumour . . . operate tomorrow.'

I thought, *bullshit, they've got the wrong bloke and the wrong X-ray.*

Right bloke.

I couldn't take this all in. He looked so ordinary. Actually he looked like one of my cousins. But this was no ordinary bloke. He was a neurosurgeon – the best, they said. I didn't really know what a brain surgeon was supposed to look like. My notion was of a tall skinny bloke, probably with a beard, about sixty-five with long thin fingers and an impossibly aloof attitude. If God was an earthly being – and a bloke – I reckon that's what he'd look like.

'We can't make any promises,' he said, 'we'll just go with the facts. Okay?'

I could only nod.

'The fact is there is no doubt this is a brain tumour.'

'Malignant?' I asked.

'We won't know definitely till we analyse it. Facts only. The tumour should be relatively easy to get at. It's also a good size to operate on. However because of where it is, your speech, comprehension and motor function could be affected.'

I'm quiet. Shock!

'We'll do our very best. No promises, but we'll look forward to a good outcome.'

The next morning I endured a terrifying preparation for a craniotomy and then I knew no more.

As I was to discover the neurosurgeon was a delightful person, just the opposite of my preconceptions. He treated the nurses and the tea lady in the same manner as he treated his peers. He was so easy to talk to, approachable and friendly.

He told me, 'You've done well. You're one of the lucky ones. Not many fare as well.'

I asked, 'What future might I have?'

'Well, how old are you again?'

'Forty-six.'

'Well, by the time you're sixty Indonesia might have invaded Australia, you might have been run over by a bus, or the tumour might have shown signs of further trouble. I know they're not facts. There is no way of knowing.'

I took that in. Another fifteen years perhaps.

'Just go and enjoy your life. There's so much more for you. Just keep taking the epilepsy tablets. They'll control any further seizures.'

I must have still looked a little doubtful.

'Just go for it. A life lived in fear is not worth living. This will become just a hiccup to you shortly – a bit of a speed bump.'

He pretended to punch me on the shoulder as he turned to leave. 'You'll be right mate.'

He left, then returned a few minutes later, putting his head around the doorway to say, 'Happy birthday.'

I'd forgotten.

He saved my life. My sort of bloke – an extraordinary Aussie if ever there was one.

I don't think I can do this. I want to go home to see if they've baled the hay. I want to see my eight working dogs and the new pups. I don't want this. What has happened to my life? Where will this end?

'Come on, Rhylle. This won't take more than a quarter of an hour. It's not too bad.'

The oncologist required a mask to be made to encase my head while I had thirty-four shots of radiotherapy, nine per fortnight.

'This is going to feel very hot. You'll think it's burning you, but it won't. Just try to relax and let us do what has to be done.'

I asked my brain to do its thirty-second blank out, but I failed to achieve my desired state.

Two of them were holding a big sheet of steaming plastic and they laid it flat on my face.

'Deep breath now and let it out slowly!'

Christ almighty! Shi-i-t! How long?

'You're all right. Hold still. Let it out slowly.'

They worked feverishly, moulding the plastic to my features. Eyes covered. God I needed another breath. Then it cooled a little. *Phew! Thank God that's over.*

Nuclear medicine it's termed. For Christ's sake, I'm not George Jetson and this is the Wesley Hospital not bloody Cape Canaveral. I couldn't believe this was me.

I'd received good news and bad news. The bad news was that my brain tumour was malignant. The good news was that malignant brain tumours rarely have secondaries.

You'll probably be dead, but at least you'll know it wasn't a second-ary that got you. Comforting thought. It was surreal. I may sound cynical, but that's possibly normal at times like these.

If the truth be known I was really thankful for a second chance and had nothing but admiration for these teams of profession-als. The therapy I was to undergo would decrease the chances of a recurrence. My head had to be completely immobilised, the custom-made mask clamped on firmly as I lay on a narrow table. I was covered with heavy lead sheeting and only then could the radio waves be administered. Each session I was returned to exactly the same position – for the thirty-four days.

Travelling an hour each way to the hospital became irksome. I suggested to Karyn that if I stuck my head in the microwave and hit the auto reheat it might save all the travel, but the idea didn't get off the ground. I think they must have let all my good ideas out when they operated on my head – I'm not sure I've had any since.

I was being reined in. My life wasn't my own. I didn't make the decisions any more. I felt like a brumby stallion, yarded for the first time in an enclosure from which there was no escape. Fighting. Battering. Rearing. Striking. Hopeless. Helpless.

Outwardly I was calm. Inwardly I was screaming. *Let me go! Let me go! Open the gate! I need to be free!* My adventurous life seemed over.

Acceptance came creeping . . .

As the treatment came to an end I was anxious to put the whole episode behind me and get on with my life. I wanted to pick up where I left off. I didn't want anything to change and there was so much to be done. I loved my life the way it was. The farm couldn't be neglected any longer.

'These tablets make me sick. I'm not taking them. It's not epilepsy anyway. They're only bits of dizzy spells.'

'Rhylle it's a small price to pay. Do as they tell you.'

'But I think I'm allergic to them.'

'You're not allergic to the tablets, you're allergic to the thought of having to take them. You should be thankful that the epilepsy led the doctors to the tumour. It saved your life, you know. Take them. I don't want you whizzing around on one ear, to use your expression.'

'Okay then.' I had no counter to that.

I did take them for a few more weeks, but by then I was feeling so well that I threw them out the window – literally. I didn't want to believe that I was an epileptic. My decision seemed to be borne out, given the complete absence of any maverick brain signals over the next six months – not a sign of a seizure. Then bang!

It could have been serious. I was sawing out fence posts from a round billet of log. In the past I'd never fallen when a seizure hit, but this time was a little different. While bent over, chainsaw in hand and running at full revs, I staggered forward as the seizure took hold. Badly shaken and consumed by the overwhelming post-seizure tiredness, I left everything where it was and retreated homewards.

I started taking the tablets again. In fact it was a different anticonvulsant medication that the doctors thought might be more suitable. Same predictable result. Feeling on top of the world. Who needs them? Out the window. According to the enclosed leaflet they didn't mix with alcohol and I didn't want my roistering lifestyle to change.

Maybe to prove how well I had recovered, I took on a substantial railway sleeper cutting contract with a partner. It was heavy work but I'd never been scared of that. It was during the hottest months of the year but the heat had never bothered me either. We met the deadline – just. Then I started to regress.

More seizures. More drug finetuning. Still I drove myself harder and harder.

'Karyn, I think we'll log Trinity out. There's still a lot of good timber that could go. It might help the finances.'

'Can't it wait for a bit? Things aren't that dire yet.'

Despite family pressure against the idea, I decided to go ahead. The local sawmill agreed to take delivery of acres of top-quality mill timber from our property and with another acquaintance I proceeded to cut, snig, and haul load after load over the range to the mill. I was reliving my early working life.

'Sawdust in my blood,' I told my wife.

'Slow down,' she replied, 'you're asking for trouble.'

Then as she turned away she said, as if to herself, 'I'm not going to worry about anything I can't change. Whatever will be, will be.'

The work *was* taking its toll on every aspect of my life.

More seizures. More finetuning, ad nauseam. The writing was clearly on the wall. Still I resisted.

'You've got to stop, Rhylle. Slow down. The money's not important.'

But nothing could stop me.

Then without warning I hit a brick wall.

Depression set in. Deeper and deeper I sank. I hated the pills.

I hated what had happened to me. I hated that I was powerless to halt the insidious forces that were changing me.

Happy pills went against my grain, but I took them. I was being brought to heel – the hard way. My run was almost halted and my spirit partly broken, acceptance slowly seeping its way into my psyche.

But it wasn't quite over yet.

A new drug, gabapentin, was prescribed. It was said to be a major breakthrough as an anticonvulsant. Not only that, it was alcohol tolerant. *That's the one for me*, I thought. However, the drug company's interpretation of alcohol tolerance must have been a little different to mine. The combined effect of an anticonvulsant, an antidepressant, alcohol, nicotine, and physical and mental stress took its toll. It flattened me. Flattened me and sent me half mad – off my head. Ambulances and sirens, emergency department, staff at a trot, drips, EEG monitors, more than forty-eight hours' intensive care, another MRI scan. A series of frightening seizures, my body twisting and contorting as I rolled from one to the next. Over a hundred seizures during a ten-day period. But I know nothing of this. I have no recollection of anything other than a continuous violent electrical storm in my head. The doctors told me I should have been dead. I nearly was.

The after-effects left me with suicidal thoughts. I realised later that during the ensuing period there was someone with me constantly. Maybe this was expected after the cocktail of drugs that they'd used to bring the seizure activity under control. Wardsmen seemed to lounge in the doorway to my cubicle. I was angry and rude and told them off. I wakened and found a nurse sitting on a chair in the doorway. I was more pleasant to her and asked how long she'd been there.

'All night; just keeping an eye on you. You threw yourself out of bed, but I doubt you remember. Do you?'

I shook my head.

'You seem more settled today. How do you feel?'

'Better, I think. I want to get out of here.'

'It's a bit soon for that,' she said quietly.

'I could jump out the window. I'd be free then.'

She gave me a startled look.

Looking at the solid sheet of glass I could almost picture myself doing it. Scary thoughts. I had been categorised as a 'survivor personality' very early in the piece. This didn't seem to fit the mould. I didn't really know if I'd jump, but the window didn't open anyway. So first chance I got when I wasn't being observed I ripped the drip from my arm, surprised myself at the amount of blood, grabbed a wad of tissues and took off for the lift.

I bolted from hospital in my pyjamas and caught a taxi home. The family was aghast. I caused a lot of trouble before another ambulance took me straight back. Chastened, I submitted.

Some time later, about a week I think, I was discharged, still somewhat dazed and weak, still full of pills. Slowly, over the next few weeks, things returned to some semblance of normal.

I was now under the close scrutiny of one of Brisbane's best neurologists – the same man who had treated me in hospital. I didn't know then who he was, nor would I have cared. At my first visit to him after that fiasco he quietly outlined what my future might be on my present course.

'You'll have to take things in check. You can change you know. It doesn't have to be bad. This isn't the only way to live a life. Lots of people have a bit of brain damage and are epileptic. For some the epilepsy is so well controlled that nobody else knows. There's only one catch. No alcohol. It has to be removed from the equation.'

'Good as done,' I said.

That was six years ago. Alcohol binges and cigarettes were already part of my past as I emerged from his consulting room, and they remain so.

I understood at last.

The neurologist has said he's delighted at the progress I've made and to him that's worth more than any money. It makes me feel good that it makes him feel good. He saved me from myself.

So what could I do with the rest of my life? My outlook was changing fast. I was powerless to stop it and for the first time I didn't even want to. Likes and dislikes were altering. My interest in the land was waning to the extent of having already disposed of part of Trinity, with similar plans in hand for the balance. The stock had already been sold off. I couldn't continue. I didn't want to continue in that direction. As Trinity was being sold off piecemeal we returned to our home town of Dayboro.

Predictably I had some time off, all the while casting about for a new direction. Karyn and I travelled around the country a bit: Uluru, Lawn Hill National Park, Perth, the newly opened and incredibly remote Diamantina Lakes National Park.

Now what?

I terraced a quarter of an acre of steep hillside with leftover railway sleepers and planted a huge vegetable garden. On another couple of acres I established a hundred native softwood trees, eventually to become a little rainforest. A chookhouse came next.

Now what?

Dan: 'Dad will you help me renovate the kitchen?'

Kylie: 'Dad will you rebuild my bathroom?'

Ben: 'Dad do you want to come fishing?' (He's a perfectionist. My work is a bit rough for him.)

Now what?

I didn't have to make the next decision. It was made for me. Another extraordinary character was about to enter my life. A little elderly bloke and his wife moved in next door. When I say next door I mean about two kilometres away.

On my way past he waved. I waved back.

Friendly old man, I thought. *Probably meet him one day soon.*

One night at a gathering only a week later I spotted him across the room. I was on my way over to say, 'Welcome to our little neck of the woods, mate.'

Karyn intercepted me and said, 'Are you going across to meet our new neighbour?'

I nodded, 'Yes, why?'

'I bet you have no idea who he is. Have a guess. I'll come with you.'

'Stop it. Who is he?'

'Does *Storm Boy* ring a bell? Or *Blue Fin*? Or *Sun on the Stubble*?'

'Bullshit! It couldn't be. They made those books into movies. He's a famous author.'

'Did you know he's Sandy's dad?'

'Colin Thiele is?'

Her turn to nod. She was grinning like the Cheshire cat.

That brilliant writer of kids books – 105 of them – is regarded as God in teaching circles.

'G'day, mate, welcome to our neck of the woods.'

That evening was the beginning of the rest of my life, my new life. I should be so lucky.

Our friendship blossomed. No, it was more than that. I called him mate and after a while he called me mate. I'm not sure if he was used to being addressed as 'mate' because at the outset he seemed a little awkward, amused perhaps. I suppose to someone who has run universities and teachers colleges it may have been a little alien.

South Australia's loss was Queensland's gain. The boy from Eudunda had moved to Dayboro next door to one of his daughters, Sandy, and not far from the other, Janne.

I had always kept a notebook of yarns that I had heard over the years, intending to do something with them one day, when I retired or some time. Colin delighted in the rollicking accounts of my own and other people's adventures, and I was similarly enthralled with the stories from this master raconteur.

'Well why don't you start writing them now? Put them together in a little anthology. You've certainly got enough material and you probably have the time as you regain your health,' he said.

That was the beginning.

Of my first attempt he could have said, 'This is shit,' because I now know it was. Or he could have said, 'Don't give up your day job. This will never earn you a cracker.'

But he didn't. What he did say was, 'Rhylle, there's a lot of good material here. You've got an engaging, racy style. Not many have the ability to record a yarn and lose nothing in the translation, or even make it better. With a severe edit these yarns might find a small niche market in rural communities.'

From the master! He even wrote a foreword for the little book, which would be the first of a trilogy. It's a wonder he agreed to put his name to it. I didn't even know I had a style.

Colin became my constant inspiration. He had severe health problems yet his joy in life was all encompassing. He laughed easily and entertained readily at age eighty-six.

Whenever I think of his love of the English language I'm first reminded of a little snippet he told me. It was about a newspaper report of troops returning from the war – I can't remember which war.

To a ticker-tape welcome the victorious troops were marching down the street in full battle dress and keeping in step with an enthusiastic military band. Impressive!

The report in the following day's edition of the newspaper described the parade in glowing terms under the headline, 'Our Boys Home at Last'.

'After such and such, followed by more of the same, added to which, then following blah blah application to bring . . . to their knees . . . here we have the battle scared *troops who fought for our continued freedom.'*

There was an uproar – 'battle scared' indeed! Major apology and voluminous retraction in the following edition.

'After such and such . . . here we have the bottle scarred *troops who fought for our freedom.'*

A couple of letters in the wrong place and a junior subeditor's career was probably stalled.

One day I asked Colin's diminutive vibrant wife Rhonda how he kept such good spirits amid such pain from severe arthritis.

'Oh, he has his ways.'

I waited.

'He has remarkable mental control. Each morning he boxes his pain and pushes the lid down hard. Then he pushes the box aside and gets on with his day. Sometimes a little seeps out – but not much.'

I felt some personal kinship. I wondered if it took him thirty seconds each morning.

Because of my history, I suppose understandably, I find visiting others in hospitals most unsettling. No, I find hospitals hard to take, not the people in them. Colin had lots of hospital stays where all sorts of body parts were restored, rebuilt, revamped and rustproofed in response to his debilitating arthritic condition. But I couldn't go and see him. Instead, I wrote a bit of nonsense and sent it in to him. He always responded.

Once I wrote:

There is this bloke named Thiele
And bloody tough he is really
With all his parts replaced
Twenty-five ops regularly spaced

Another bloke he is nearly.

He replied:

> *There was a young man from Eudunda*
> *Whose trousers fell off him from under*
> *When facing arrest*
> *He cried out distressed*
> *But my belt simply parted asunder.*

Another time I wrote:

> *I know this old geezer from Eudunda*
> *Who can write up a storm like thunder*
> *His pen is his sword*
> *He's won every award*
> *No blunders for the Eudunda wonder.*

And he replied:

> *Professor Albert Alpenstocks*
> *Wears open ended shoes and socks*
> *Which allow him weekly without fuss*
> *To trim his toenails in the bus.*

He continued to encourage me – goad me if I became sidetracked. He did a little editing for me and became my sometime professional reader who gave me honest opinions. Nine books later he was still guiding me, from my early rather embarrassing attempts to the later works that received good reviews. None of it would have happened without Colin Thiele. Or if it had, I wonder if it would have fizzled out. I got the impression that he gained some small pleasure out of my modest success. He's gone now and I miss him.

I couldn't believe it. A Sydney publisher sent plane tickets and a book of taxi vouchers. 'We would like you here for a promo round. We've got some TV and radio interviews booked for you. You will stay at the Siebel.'

'Christ Almighty,' I said to Karyn, 'can you believe it? The Siebel is five stars. I'll tell them I'm only a three-star bloke and ask if I can have the rest of the money instead.'

'You've earned it. Enjoy it. I'll cash in my fly-buys and come with you.'

And on that first trip she did. It was wonderful.

I think back and I marvel. Not long ago I was driving tractors and chasing cattle – a lout from the backblocks. Now I'm writing books and people seem to want more. My life is very ordered these days. Regular mealtimes and regular pill popping, plenty of sleep and absolutely no stress. And never have I been happier. I've kept most of my old friends and have dozens of new ones. They're from another walk of life – people to do with publishing, writers' festivals, workshops, seminars and other areas of the arts. And they are very different. Almost to a tee they are unreliable, all are free spirited and free thinkers, all have unfettered minds. I think I'm becoming one of them, as far as unreliability, that is.

Two lives in the one lifetime. I should be so lucky.

OSCAR NEILSON
When the chips are down . . .

———•◆•———

Many days I worked for Oscar and many more I worked beside him in my own business, though in later years, we mostly sat and talked. He used to be tanned, fit and strong – now in his eighties he was pale, weak and frail, but although his body was failing, his mind was not. In the wheelchair he hated so much, he relived his life in our long afternoon conversations on the verandah of the nursing home. What I didn't glean of his life story as I worked with him, I did as we sat and talked. Some of it I have had to piece together, like the story he'd told me about his father.

'Hear that, young fella?' Tad had asked his son. 'Listen hard and remember that sound.'

He'd whacked the trunk of the blue gum hard with the back of his axe. 'You know what, son? That tree is hollow. And there's a family of possums living in one of those limbs.'

Oscar looked incredulous, 'How do you know the limbs are hollow? How can you see right up there. You didn't even look.'

'By the dead twigs right out on the ends of the branches. They're hollow all right. And see here?' Tad pointed, 'This possum wasn't in a hurry as he climbed up, but look at these other claw marks. Something was after this bloke as *he* went up. See how deep the marks are and how they're gouged out of the bark – and how far apart they are too, compared with the first one?'

The lesson had continued. 'Here're the tracks of the dingo that treed the second possum,' he said, pointing. 'That only happened last night. She'd be a bitch with new pups this time of year – hungry as hell.'

'Yeah?'

'That sap is still wet where it's been oozing out of the possum's claw marks,' he pointed again, dabbing his finger in it. 'It's not long since it stopped dripping, so it would have been early this morning. The poor bloody possum was probably on his way home with a full belly. I bet he got a fright,' and Oscar would have laughed.

A little further on, Tad swung the back of his axe at the bole of another blue gum. 'Bloody hollow too. They'll all be hollow along this side of the ridge. We'll go around to the northern slope.'

Over the top, the next tree he hit with his axe gave a dull thud, 'Now we're in business. See how the canopy is all healthy and green – no dead twigs?'

'Any possums in this one, Dad?'

And Tad had answered, 'You should be able to tell.'

In the '30s, most Australian households were struggling and Oscar's family was no different. Depression still had the country on its knees and recovery seemed a long way off. Forced to leave school at age ten to help with the family budget, Oscar was expected to work like a man from that day onwards. There were five sisters and twin brothers in the family. He was the fifth born – the first male child. Small contribution he might have made, but it was needed. So by age eleven he was working beside his father, squaring off house stumps with a heavy broadaxe – and in their spare time they cut five or six cords of wood weekly, stacks each approximately five-foot square, mostly for the half a dozen bakeries within range. Oscar's everyday work axe was similar to his father's; a full-size tool, well worn and perhaps a little lighter because of it. Weather-dried black wattle and red oak – two of the hardest and densest timbers in the bush – were the only species acceptable to the bakers for their burning provided a lasting, even heat. It wasn't long before the child-man knew every patch in the district.

All those around him predicted he would become a professional timber-getter, so diligent and efficient had he become about his work. That prophecy was to come true, but in fact he had little option; he knew nothing else. His four cousins, themselves brothers, were all timber-getters in the forests nearby, and it seemed a natural progression.

Self-reliant and capable, Oscar preferred to work alone; although each morning he employed an offsider to partner him on the crosscut saw. His work environment was south-east Queensland's eucalypt woodlands, and the forest claimed him as one of its own. Any part of it – scrub-covered misty mountain range, steep slippery gorge, sunlit savannah or creek flat – saw him comfortable, in tune and at ease.

'Get out of the way, old boy, or I'll run over you. What's that big lump in your guts? Looks like you ate half a wallaby,' Oscar would say to the big sluggish carpet python trying to warm up in the first sun of the winter morning. 'Christ almighty, do I have to go back and come out on the other track? The bloody things a man does for you,' and he'd back up. Such was the bushman that the snake had equal rights.

'And you bastards shut up too or I'll bring the shotgun back next load,' he'd say to a trio of screeching black cockatoos as they alighted in a blue gum overhead. 'Ah well, I suppose you live here too, you cheeky buzzards. Hope you brought the rain with you.'

The pattern to his work day seldom varied. The morning was spent dropping enough selected trees, which, when cut into log lengths would make up a load. His practised techniques and methodical strokes were deceptive. How effortless he made it look. As the saw bit deeper he'd bump a wedge in behind it, just for safety's sake. 'Timber-r-r!'

He told me he'd loaded the old truck and trailer a thousand times. And then came a loading he'd never forget. On this particular day, the first log was a big tallowwood – pushed hard up against the chocks on the far side – with another of smaller diameter on the bed beside it and lastly, a stringybark on the near side to match the size and length of the first. A balanced load so far. Then Oscar loaded two shorter ironbarks, not quite the same length as each other, on top, though well forward to throw most of their weight over the drive wheels of the truck. These he wedged into the vees between the bed logs, which spread them against the chocks – a full, even and compact load.

The chains were a formality – one each at the front and rear, and a lighter belly chain around the middle, all tightened to incredible tautness with turn buckles. This load, like all the others, would never move during transport – even without the chains. Loading completed, Oscar proceeded to the mill, 8 miles away.

As Oscar recounted his story it wasn't hard for me to picture the events – coming from a timber family it was just so ordinary. At the mill he began unloading. He made it look so easy – professionals always make it look that way. After letting the tension off, the front and rear chains were unhooked and thrown down into the growing heap beside the toolbox. Knocking the pins out of the chocks was a little more strenuous. There was very little danger with the rear chock as the other would still hold the load. Even so, there was plenty of tension on it and when Oscar hit it with the sledgehammer the pin flew out behind, almost the same distance as the length of the jinker. The second pin then held all the weight. After a sharp whack with the hammer, the pin came only partway free.

'Bastard of a thing.' Slam! Oscar hit it again. Still jammed. After a lot of bother it came free. With the last hit the chock flew out behind, landing almost on top of the first one.

Oscar ducked in under the load still on the truck – a safe spot and the usual practice – and undid the belly chain. As the tension came off, the load suddenly shifted and one of the top logs dropped down between the two nearest bed logs, but missed catching the rear cross bolster by an inch. At the last millisecond Oscar realised he'd made the slightest miscalculation.

'Look out, Oscar! Look out!' Roy Dickfos, the mill proprietor, yelled.

The short end of the ironbark instantly dropped through the gap and caught Oscar across the shoulder. As it pushed him forward, it tore through his shirt, scraped down his spine and crumpled his body. Bare sinew and bone were exposed from the base of his neck to his tailbone. Then the log rolled, crushed his leg and stopped half a turn clear of him.

'Aa-a-rgh!'

Then silence.

'Mate, just stay where you are! Just hang on, please hang on! We'll get help as soon as we can. It might be better not to move. Could do more damage.' Oscar told me later that Roy had spoken in near panic.

'Can't do much else other than hang on, can I? Not much bloody chance of moving either. Get my waterbottle out of the cab.'

He was face down, sheet white and sweating profusely.

'Oscar, too much water won't do you any good. Just wet your lips and mouth mate.'

'A man's dying of thirst.'

'No, Oscar. You shouldn't.'

So he didn't.

The ambulance bearers were quiet and careful as they did what they had to do, but Oscar told me that their looks had said everything – his case seemed hopeless. Most of his body had taken the weight of the log, to a greater or lesser extent. His back was a hideous mess and one leg was turned sideways with bone protruding – his laboured breathing bubbled blood, indicating rib and lung damage. Internal injuries were the main worry.

It took two hours before Oscar was admitted to the Royal

Brisbane Hospital. He'd had no pain-killers – nor had he asked for any. He'd made no complaint or sound. In his eyes, a broken body didn't equate with a broken spirit. His injuries were horrific: broken back – thankfully leaving the spinal cord intact – broken shoulder (half of it beyond repair); broken pelvis; broken hip; broken leg; five broken ribs; punctured lung and an extensive serious flesh wound. I'm sure his friends and family wondered how he could survive.

Lying in that hospital bed, almost completely covered in plaster and bandages, Oscar's drugged mind began drifting back and forth over his youth. He told me that he couldn't explain the flashbacks he experienced at that time, but that he could still recall them vividly fifty years later. In one of the flashbacks, Oscar was fourteen years old again. It was 1935 and the best of Australia's east coast wood-choppers, plus a few New Zealanders, were gathered at Lawnton Showgrounds in south-east Queensland. Oscar said, 'I can still see it, you know, after all these years. I was there early and watched the other axemen coming in. I don't think many of them knew who I was. I bet they didn't know I would be cutting against them. Some of them got there early to get the best spots – half in the ring some of them. A couple of the big, useless buggers complained if they had to park away a bit because it was too far to lug their axe boxes. One of them was big enough to hold a bull out to piss one-handed, and he couldn't carry an axe box? All piss and wind.'

'I know a few blokes like that,' I said.

'Him and his mate spent a lot of time inspecting the blocks, as if they knew a lot about the game. Neither of them looked like they'd know an axe from a crowbar.'

'How'd they go?' I asked.

'Neither of them chopped a place all day. But at the start they complained that the wood was full of grub holes.'

'Was it?'

'Yeah, but I heard Bill tell them that we all had to chop the same wood.'

'What did they say to that?'

'Nothing. Then Bill told 'em that because of the holes they'd have less wood to chop. Bill laughed and they got the shits – they had no idea he was the chief steward.'

Oscar's mind must have been on a knife edge, teetering, but he told me that the showground scene seemed almost real as it replayed before him. He said he could actually smell the sawdust, and freshly cut timber; see the cut blocks and the clean-up boys pushing barrows; and hear axes ringing and the sound of the announcer's monotonous voice.

Late arrivals drew chiacking.

'Early for tomorrow, eh? Sorry, mate, they've just run your heat.'

'Piss off. Move that box and let a man in.'

'What? Last to get here and you demand the best spot? Down the end is your place,' came the light-hearted reply as the mate dragged his box sideways to make room.

The axemen sat on their boxes – rows of white singlets atop white trousers and white sandshoes. Oscar laughed as he said they had always reminded him of White Leghorn roosters lined up on a perch. Early spectators seated on long planks mirrored the image. They'd secured the best vantage points and earned withering glances as they barred a spot for the wife.

The air of expectancy was electric, nearly bubbling over – for spectators and axemen alike. Whole families had travelled with their sportsmen husbands, brothers and sons. Brothers chopped against brothers, fathers against sons, fathers and sons together in relays.

Most of the local competition axemen knew of the Neilson lad who wore a calico cap the same as his dad's. Some had seen him as a small boy watching the axemen in action. A couple had asked him if he wanted to compete when he was old enough, but none had expected to see his name on the list of that particular day's program.

Oscar knew that not one amongst them gave him any chance, but they gave him good-natured advice anyway.

Upon noticing the unfamiliar name on the list of nominations and inquiring about the new competitor, the visiting axemen thought it was some kind of joke when Oscar was pointed out to them. Newcomers were always of interest, and demanded close scrutiny. Most axemen prided themselves on knowing nearly every face on the circuit.

One stranger was heard to say, 'Woodchopping isn't a sport for kids. I don't know why the hell they let him even nominate; he can't be more than twelve at the outside. Ruin a bloody good sport letting kids drop the standard. Scraping the bottom of the barrel if you ask me.'

Oscar said his axe probably looked like it was his father's discard, because it was. He was using an Otway Chief. None of the younger men had even heard of an Otway, let alone seen one, and some were quite interested, examining it before graciously handing it back to Oscar.

'It makes a mockery of the competition – a bloody farce,' the detractor muttered.

'Axemen, you've got five minutes till event number four, first heat of the Lawnton Produce Handicap,' the announcer droned on, reading out the list of names. 'Please rig your blocks for the twelve-inch standing handicap. Open class fourteen years and over.'

The event attracted seven competitors, including two or three top-line nominations. As they all drove in dozens of nails to fix their blocks to the dummies, they watched each other like hawks, trying to get a look at the choice of axe for the event and what sort of block the opposition had drawn. The expectation was that the contest would be between two of the division-one axemen.

This meeting was the highly regarded runner-up to the state championships to be held at the Royal National Association's Brisbane grounds. Most of the choppers made final adjustments to the tail end of their training programs at this meeting, to be ready for the big one the following month at the RNA.

Oscar's father had helped him rig his block. The only adjustment Oscar had made was to give the old Otway Chief an extra rub and go to bed early the night before. From his photos, I could see he was a skinny stripling, but fit, work-hardened and determined. I knew that even though he couldn't afford a racing axe, he'd had everything else going for him. A maturing frame indicated that he would grow to be a big, powerful man. Oscar said he didn't take any notice of the jibes about his ancient axe; he knew how to use it. It was his everyday work axe. If anything their teasing only strengthened his resolve.

The twelve-inch standing was a popular event. A couple of

burly competitors huffed and puffed noisily as they tried to psyche themselves up and browbeat the competition. Some practised slow, controlled air swings. And others just breathed hard through pursed lips, looking self-conscious. Most disconcerting of all, however, was the nonchalance of the top-line trio who seemed to find something of interest away on the horizon.

Oscar told me that one of the visiting axemen had asked him how he'd go.

'I dunno, I've never done it before, not competition anyway, but I've watched them a lot and practised every day at work. I can cut a cord of baker's wood faster than anybody else around here if that makes any difference,' Oscar had replied as he adjusted his cap.

'Good luck, young fellow. They're a wonderful bunch of blokes, these woodchoppers. But they won't concede you an inch, nor should they.'

'I won't be giving them an inch either if I get in front, I can tell you.'

'Axemen, stand to your logs!'

A hush descended.

'One two —' with the call of three Oscar's axe hit the block. If he'd been a thousandth of a second earlier it would have been a false start. With the count of six, two more were away; then seven, another three; and at ten the back marker drove his first cut.

The onlookers couldn't believe the lad in the calico cap. He flew through the front of his block. Heavy chips scattered as he took plenty of wood out. He was the first to turn. He knew then that he was well ahead – and he'd taken more than half out of the front. As he drove the block off, with extreme downward accuracy and force, the last three cuts he drove down the back perfectly matched the last three he'd driven up the front.

He won that heat by a long margin. Oscar said the other men reeled with shock – he'd upset all their plans. As I listened to his story, it dawned on me that Oscar had inadvertently trained every day while he worked, but the competition hadn't. And white gum was a local species that Oscar knew well. Perhaps these two factors gave him some small advantage.

Bill Fry had watched Oscar's heat. He wouldn't have missed it for quids. Bill was renowned for his sweeping swing and the light footwork of a boxer – making him the champion he was. He was one of the few who knew young Oscar well. As the lad stepped back from the block, Bill stepped forward and shook hands with the smiling youth who was, at that moment, holding his old work axe high above his head in acknowledgment of the crowd's roar. They'd never seen a heat like it. Oscar said his father, Tad, stood quietly, giving him a slight smile and almost imperceptible nod that said it all: Well done, son, but I expected nothing less.

'What happened then?' I asked my old grey-haired mate, as we sat on the nursing home verandah.

'Well, Bill came over and tried to say something, but I couldn't hear him because the crowd was still making a racket. He had to say it three or four times before I could hear it. He told me I had a big future if I stuck with the woodchopping, but that I needed a new axe. I wasn't used to praise, but Bill sure gave me some. I tell you, it was one of the highlights of my life.'

'I bet it made some of them look a bit stupid. A lad comes in with his woodheap axe and whips the arse off a few of the big boys.'

'Ah no, it was only a heat, but it felt pretty good.'

He went on, 'Bill said I would be up against some of the best in the final, some of the best in Australia and New Zealand. For a moment I'd forgotten about the final. Then it hit me like a brick. I remember shaking my head in disbelief.'

Oscar was quiet for a moment, lost in the past perhaps, then went on.

'Bill beckoned me to come with him. I followed but had no idea what he wanted. We only went 20 yards and he stopped in front of his axebox. He reached in and pulled one out and handed it to me. As I unstrapped its cover I started to realise what he had in mind. My heart missed a beat I can tell you.'

'What sort of an axe was it?'

'A bloody Plum, his best axe.'

'He told me to take it and use it in the final, that it would suit my style. He was a good bit heavier than me, but our styles weren't that much different you know. He said I could give some of these blokes, including himself, a bit of a run for their money. 'High praise, that was,' Oscar said. 'I didn't even know I had a style.'

'I told Bill I couldn't use it. It was his best axe and he'd need it in the final. What if I gapped it? I couldn't afford another one to replace it.'

But Bill had insisted.

As the time for the final approached, Oscar said he was nearly jumping out of his skin with anticipation and barely controlled nervous energy. Some of the best in Australia and New Zealand – he could barely believe it. He was fourteen, his first open chop, and he was up against the best in the sport. Wow!

Bill was back marker in the same event. Oscar was to go at the count of three in recognition of the fact that he was chopping in open company, or any company, for the first time and, of course, hadn't earned a handicap yet. Bill was out on eleven seconds.

Technically, going on past performance and ability these axemen should have all finished together – if the handicapper had done his job, and if the choppers were at their usual standard. Some of the other old hands had joked that Bill might regret lending that beautifully prepared Plum to the Neilson lad. He might beat the lot of them – especially after what they'd witnessed in the heat. But then, others reasoned, he might have over-stretched himself in the heat and mightn't have anything left for the final. After all he was still only a slight youngster – not much to draw on in either body or experience.

They were all competition-hardened axemen. No, Oscar knew that he was still an outsider because even though he'd won the heat he had drawn the best block in that event. They had inspected the cut block and agreed it was perfect wood – but then so were the axe marks in it. Oscar had definitely rattled some of them.

I imagined the announcer interrupting Oscar's thoughts. '. . . final of the twelve-inch standing handicap. Axemen stand to your logs. One, two, three —' Oscar probably didn't hear the rest.

In a blur of speed his axe flew through the front of his block, chewing out huge chips. He'd changed sides and put a couple of cuts in the back before Bill turned . . . after having overtaken the rest of the field even though he'd been the back marker. Oscar's axe bit into the second side with the speed and accuracy usually displayed only by top axemen – but he was tiring fast. He was running on heart – nothing else. He was fully spent as he drove the block off with three sweeping downward strokes that were perfectly judged. He couldn't have swung another blow.

He'd won by one and a half seconds! He said elation and excitement had surged through him and then a quick pang of guilt that he'd beaten Bill.

The crowd's roar went unheeded. He was completely done in – hardly able to catch his breath. I pictured him there, barely able to stand without the stump for support, feeling sick to the pit of his stomach as disbelief flooded over him. What had he just done? Momentarily numb, he stood – recovering by degrees and still drawing huge breaths as he examined the edge of the perfectly balanced axe in his rough young hands.

'I asked Bill if he'd let me win,' said Oscar. 'But he said "No bloody fear." He'd only cut that time once or twice in his whole life. He said I won it fair and square and that I should enjoy it a bit – the bloody crowd went wild.'

That was the start of a magnificent career and Bill's words and kind gesture had helped launch it.

Oscar started his career by winning that event in the championship style that was to become expected of him in the future. It had never before been recorded that a fourteen-year-old had won an 'Open' chop – let alone in A-class company – at his first attempt, and one who didn't even own a racing axe.

His first handicap penalised him three seconds, but as it turned out it was little handicap. Each successive win pegged him back till he was back marker in nearly every handicap event he entered. That didn't stop him. He said he didn't see it as an imposition – more a personal challenge. In the championships, he won most events because all axemen started off the count of three.

As he matured he continued with the sport which was an extension of his work. He quickly became a champion in all other events for which he'd nominated – the underhand, and springboard events necessitating the climbing of both sides of the tree on three lifts of the boards then cutting halfway through from each side. But his favourite was always the twelve-inch standing – that same event he'd won as a fourteen-year-old.

I'd called to see Oscar at the nursing home hoping he might tell me more about the aftermath of the logging accident that had almost claimed his life. It was a wet July afternoon, unusual for that time of year.

As I waited for someone to come to reception I looked down towards the big central hall where most of the social activities took place. I could see two rows of oldies, seated each side of a long table. After stating the purpose of my visit, I made my way down to the table. As I neared it I scanned the faces, trying to find Oscar, but I should have known. He was in the wheelchair facing away from me. He was the caller for the bingo.

When I spoke, he recognised my voice and wheeled around in greeting, completely deserting his post and leading me off towards the verandah.

'Oscar, what about the game?'

'Bugger the game, I can play that anytime.'

'What about the others?'

'Somebody will take over.'

Normally we would sit in the sun or shade at either end of the verandah, but that day I suggested we stay indoors.

'No, boy. I like it outside. I like the rain.'

'And the wind?'

He nodded and said, 'If I could get out of this bloody contraption I'd be out there in it. You know a bit of rain never stopped us before, did it?'

After we got settled he recalled that dreadful recovery time.

'I was only thirty when it happened. You probably know that – 1951.'

I nodded.

'I didn't know how long I'd been out to it, but when I came to properly, I realised that I was a bit buggered.'

'Just a bit, Oscar? A fair bit, wasn't it?'

'I think they were pumping me full of pain-killers because I didn't feel too bad. I was covered in plaster, and face down a lot of the time, but I could put up with it.'

I just shook my head. *Talk about tough.*

'They reckoned I mightn't walk again. I told them to go to buggery. Then another doctor told me I might be in a bloody wheelchair. I told him to go to buggery too. I'm in one now, but for fifty years after I got crushed I wasn't.'

Once again he shifted awkwardly in the chair. I could tell by his expression that he was in pain. My heart went out to him.

'They told me I had a right to know and that they had a duty to tell me. One bloke said my injuries were simply too extensive.

I told them that I didn't need that bullshit and if they could get me upright I'd do the rest.'

'What did they say to that?'

'Only that they'd give me their best attention, but no promises.'

I nodded again.

He continued, 'When they started physio they were too soft on me. I told them to get stuck into it, don't be playing around. I said I'd tell them if I couldn't stand it. So they got fair dinkum, and slowly I got a bit better.'

Six months after his accident he was walking, nine months afterwards he was back at work cutting cord wood, at ten months competing in standing and underhand woodchop events, and at eleven months winning the tree events. The fact that he'd been extremely fit saved him, the doctors said. Never had they met anyone so determined nor witnessed any recovery like it. He'd stunned everyone, except, perhaps, the woodchopping fraternity and those in the local timber industry who'd known for a long while that he was made of stern stuff.

Oscar went on to regain his place at the very top of the sport, in all events, and no other axeman could come within a bull's roar of him for many years. They'd come from everywhere: choppers familiar with east coast timbers of New South Wales and Victoria, some of the very best timbermen from the wild ranges and gorges of Tasmania, choppers from the giant timber forests of Western Australia, whole parties of New Zealand champions, and smaller groups of Americans who had absolutely no knowledge of Australian hardwoods. If they didn't come to him he went to them, travelling all over Australia with Bill Fry. Nowhere could they handle Oscar Neilson.

The Queensland Branch of the Australian Axemen's Association had elected Oscar to the committee when he was twenty-eight, and he was still there fifty-six years later. He didn't do things by halves. For eighty years (forty as a competitor) Oscar had attended every Lawnton meeting, and every RNA competition, except for a couple during the war. In later years he was still organising, delegating, and sometimes overseeing the entire program. He said often that one of the most important jobs he had on the day was looking after the ring crew – the clean-up blokes on the rakes and barrows. He meant that. He made each of us feel as important as any champion axemen, fussing around making sure we had lunch, that we had enough help, and that our water bottles were full. No detail was missed.

One day he beckoned the boss of the ring crew to him. 'Now I want you to tell your boys to be bloody careful they don't get those cut blocks mixed up. Keep the piles well apart. Make sure they can tell the difference between white gum and this swamp mahogany. You're responsible for that.'

'Okay, Oscar. They do all know the difference, but I'll still keep an eye on them.'

'Good. Normally I wouldn't mix the two species for the one meeting but this mahogany was handy, and it's only for a couple of events. Good wood to cut, though. They all like it.'

After the show, every year, he'd spend the next couple of days delivering the waste white gum to every pensioner in the district who needed firewood. No charge. The odd bottle of beer, maybe, but never a shilling changed hands. And there wasn't a single block of mahogany in any load because it doesn't burn well.

It wasn't just the ring crew he looked after. Oscar never forgot his beginnings. He helped run the Lawnton woodchopping program for many years, and also supplied all the timber for this and two other meetings in the shire (Dayboro and Samford), sizing most of the blocks with his trusty broadaxe. Oscar and his mate, Ted Protheroe, could be seen toiling away for a fortnight before the meeting, swinging the heavy broadaxes day after day. That was after the four or five days sourcing, cutting, snigging, loading and carting the logs to work on. They were true sportsmen; money wasn't the motivation

In his career as a top-notch axeman he won 3251 ribbons and next to no prize money to go with them. I still have clippings from a 1960s *Courier-Mail* that show Oscar preparing for one of his many competitions: in one photograph he's standing beside his father Tad, wearing his calico cap, in another he's admiring the edge on his favourite axe, and in another, shaving with it.

When he was eighty years old, I sat with him watching the contractors preparing the blocks for the Lawnton Show. He slowly shook his head. They were using a big wood lathe to pare the blocks down to size. The result was perfect, every time.

He didn't say, 'Ah, we did it the old way with the broadaxe.'

He didn't say, 'Ah, we had it a lot tougher back in my day.'

He didn't say, 'Ah, you blokes are getting soft.'

He did say, 'Ah, wish to Christ we'd had one of them sixty years ago.'

Sadly, Oscar passed away in January 2006, surrounded by his family. I'd been to see him in hospital only a few days before. When I'd asked him how he was he'd answered, 'I'd rather be out in the paddock. I'm buggered now. You make sure that you keep that woodchop going. I'm bloody proud of you, boy.'

He was referring to my ten years in charge of the woodchop-ping program at Dayboro, another little town in the same shire as Lawnton. Together we'd built it into the most highly regarded woodchop meeting in Queensland, outside the Royal. He was as proud as I was.

At his funeral, upon entry to the church each mourner was handed two prize-winning ribbons. We were invited to keep one as a memento if we wished and to drop the other on his coffin in the grave.

For me it was a personal farewell, mate to mate. Oscar had done it for my dad, and for my timber-getting uncles. Now it was my turn.

Saluté! Oscar Richard Neilson, Champion of Champions – the lad with the Otway Chief and the calico cap.

RAY DAHL
Man for all seasons

———•◆•———

'**H**ere, put this in the tape deck,' Ray said, taking a new cassette from his top pocket and handing it to me. 'I picked it up this week.'

'Who is it?' I asked as I flicked on the interior light. 'Slim?'

'You'll see.'

I was spot-on with my guess – it was a cassette of Slim Dusty's that I hadn't heard before.

'It's all right, isn't it,' I commented after twenty minutes.

'Yeah, as good as the best of his others I think. Or better. There's a couple of tracks there I really like. "Leave him in the Longyard". What did you think of that one?'

'It could be old Slim's best, I reckon. It's a bloody beauty,' I answered, smiling to myself. Any song about horses would have Ray's approval, and a Slim Dusty song about an old stockhorse was right up his alley.

After work every other Friday night, Ray and I would take off to Ocean View, our island cattle property in Central Queensland. Scrubbers, brumbies and some of our quiet cattle inhabited this wild country, five hundred odd kilometres north of our homes near Brisbane.

As a choice for a fifty-fifty arrangement there couldn't have been anyone better than Ray. A former surfie, he's tall and muscular, with strong chiselled features, although the blond hair had changed hue a little. Still raw boned, lean and fit as a fiddle, he's a capable and totally reliable business partner. Ray's the kind of bloke who leaves everything where he drops it, and puts big handfuls of herbs and spices in the spaghetti bolognaise, laughing when it gives everyone the trots within the hour.

'Had a bastard of a day today,' Ray began. 'We've got a union dispute on our hands and I've got to go in and bat for our company. It's before the Commission. I was in there all bloody day yesterday as well, and have to go in again on Monday. The rest of the job isn't too bad, but the court bit gives me the shits. I keep telling the big boss I'm a friggin' glazier not a bloody lawyer.'

'Good to get away from it all then.'

'I'd rather be busting my guts building stockyards than talking that crap. I think we'll win though. There's been trouble brewing for a while now.'

This legal battle had me intrigued, but I was still a bit in the dark.

'Is there any way of negotiating a settlement?' I asked.

'Yeah, that's what we're trying to do, but their advocate is a bastard.'

I nodded.

Ray went on, 'Project costs can easily blow out and make the difference between a profit and a disaster. The boss said he'd budgeted and quoted on an estimated 3 per cent pay rise, but the union's claim could put it way over that. Anyhow, I should get off the subject. I've been totally focused on it all week. Hey, I've got that plan for the yards done. We could start getting a bit of timber together this weekend. What do you reckon?'

I was momentarily thrown – I was still helping him fight the unions. A quick turnabout was needed here.

'Okay. We should have a good look at the lay of the land and see which way the cattle run. I think I know a good site. It's not far from China Bay, a bit past Birkenhead and on that watercourse that runs off into the mudflats.'

'Great minds mate, great minds. The tracks all converge there, not far from water. We could be on them and have them yarded before they could say "moo".'

'Which is cow language for "Jack Robinson",' I added.

Ray might have smiled in the dark, I think. Conversation lulled as the kilometres slipped by and Slim sang country ballads in his inimitable style.

After calling into Miriamvale pub for our standard two pots of beer we hit the road again feeling somewhat rejuvenated – for a while. The long drive after a full week's work was starting to take its toll.

It was about 10.30 p.m. as we pulled into our regular campsite on the Boyne River only 20 kilometres from where we'd catch the ferry in the morning. We collapsed into our swags and slept the sleep of the dead.

Breakfast at Benaraby truck stop was followed by a scramble to get down to Gladstone's O'Connell wharf to board the *Calypso* on time.

A rough crossing looked imminent because it was blowing hard even as we left the protected Calliope River mouth. A stiff south-easter facing into a strong ebb tide was a recipe for almost impossible conditions. We could only imagine what might lie ahead as we crossed Gladstone Harbour's deep shipping channel, dredged to take 200 000-tonne bauxite carriers.

Huge breakers seemed out of place in the protected waters of the harbour. The sturdy little *Calypso* had its work cut out for it, but we were confident in the abilities of the taciturn skipper.

'Ray, how would you go surfing down some of these?' I said, as a towering wall of water threatened to engulf us.

'Not too good from down here,' he answered.

Then, as the ferry rose to top the crest, 'But pretty good from up here.'

He was very much at home in the water. I wasn't.

'I remember when I was a nipper in the surf club. King's Beach at Caloundra was like this once and some of the older blokes had to take a surfboat through the breakers to get to some bloody galah outside the flags. One of our blokes nearly got drowned saving the bloody idiot.'

'Were you ever in a crew?'

'Later, yeah – we won a lot of titles. Saved a lot of people too. I spent most of my weekends at the club when I was a young lout. It was a great scene back then. We had to keep fit though.'

Just then the *Calypso* took a wave almost broadside and heeled. Ray and I could have gone below and stayed dry, but the view was fantastic, if scary, up on the open top deck – as long as we hung on tight. Not only that, if she heeled too far and capsized, I figured we would have a chance of getting thrown clear. Ray might survive, but I'd end up in a mudcrab's guts before I hit the bottom.

The seas dropped off after we'd cleared the channel, and as we chugged into the lee of a neighbouring island the water was reasonably calm although the breeze was still stiff.

'Bit better now, eh,' I said to Ray.

He simply nodded – probably lost in thoughts of his youth.

Even throttled back, the little wooden ferry cruised easily towards Curtis Island's kilometre-long jetty, which rose out of the water like a sun-bleached whale skeleton.

Sliding in slightly sideways with the motor cut to an idle, the *Calypso* docked heavily and held fast with the force of the still-pushing south-easter. Quickly we grabbed our gear. Low tide meant a heavily laden crawl up the jetty's twenty aluminium steps.

We collected our ute from our friend's backyard in the sleepy settlement of Southend. The township comprised a hundred or so holiday shacks and weekenders, some ramshackle, some more substantial. Dogs outnumbered a handful of permanent residents. A solar-powered phone box sat isolated on the esplanade facing east, a poor excuse for a lighthouse. We fuelled up at the little store and headed off. Just a couple of hundred metres north of the township we crossed the unfenced boundary between the town and our lease. Everyone in the village had permission to go through our lease on their way over to the western side of the island, mostly to go crabbing. They all knew the basic rule of the bush – to leave gates as they found them.

Two 4000-hectare paddocks made up our lease. They were almost totally surrounded by expansive mudflats, a sort of no-man's land – innocuous-looking, but deadly. From time to time animals entered the shallow tidal channels in search of the nutritious nuts that grow on the white mangroves. Between the high and low tide water marks, which delineate nature's boundary fence, they stood helpless, bogged to their bellies in a bottomless mud pit, finally succumbing to sheer exposure to the elements. A ghastly death in an unforgiving country.

As we approached our camp, 4 kilometres from the township, the four saddle horses emerged from the shade of the stunted blue gum scrub at the far end of the forty hectare flat. The bell around the blue horse's neck ding-donged in time with his footsteps. As the little company came closer the bell picked up pace, becoming more of a dong-dong-dong-dong. They knew that our arrival meant a bag of workhorse mix and a spray for mozzies and sandflies. It would have been nice to think they'd come just to see us, but without the grain and the drum of Aerogard I don't think we'd register even a passing interest. Their habit of reappearing at the camp at dawn after a rainy night, hoping to get another spray to replace the dose that had been washed off, was very endearing. But once again, as soon as we'd do that for them they would mizzle off without even a thankyou.

The horses weren't confined to the flat, but rarely strayed off it. We wondered why they didn't roam over the whole four thousand hectares – perhaps the brumbies had allocated this territory to them. A single gelding might have been tolerated in a brumby harem – but four, probably not.

On arrival we were always slightly anxious until we'd established that all was as it should be. Today our fears were ill-founded. Gear unloaded, we caught the horses, fed them and locked them in the horse yard. The morning was spent cutting rails and posts for the planned yards. Saddling up after lunch we rode out to decide on a site for the stockyards, full of anticipation. Ray had shod the horses the previous fortnight, and after generous helpings of work-horse mix and corn, both horses were nearly jumping out of their skins, raring to go. *They* thought they were going mustering. But as we were sussing out the lay of the land and would probably cover thirty or forty kilometres in the afternoon, they'd have to muster energy not cattle.

Ray was aboard the not-so-trusty Hughenden, and I rode the elegant and quickly improving thoroughbred chestnut, Cheeky, who'd been sacked from the racetrack because he was a chase horse not a racehorse. If Ray hadn't seen the chestnut's potential as a stockhorse, he wouldn't have rescued him from the Corbould Park track at Caloundra that day, and the hapless animal would have been greyhound tucker within three days of the meeting.

Because of his racetrack connections as clerk of the course, Ray had been responsible for supplying the horses for our island adventure and I trusted his judgment completely. A couple of our best stockhorses were ex-racehorses.

'Do many chase horses go straight to the knackery from the track?'

'Not many. Probably only six or seven in the ten years I was red-coating. Some of the poor buggers never had a chance. Often enough it was the bloody trainer's fault, not the horse's. The bastard that trained Cheeky couldn't train a passionfruit vine.'

We'd become quite a mustering team, Cheeky and I. Ray and

Hughenden had something special between them too – or something between them anyhow. Most often I couldn't fathom just what it was.

'That rotten bastard. Just when a man thinks he's got a real mate the mongrel ducks his head and tries to offload you. He'll do it even after a full day's mustering too, when he should be rooted. Shit he's smart. Not many like him. Bloody good horse, but a real arsehole.'

'Don't listen to him, Hughenden. Put your hooves over your ears. Make up your mind, Ray. Do you love him or do you hate him?'

'Day about.'

I'd heard about these love–hate relationships.

Even though Hughenden had missed out in the looks department he did have ability.

Ray threatened him, 'If you don't behave, I'll send you to the doggers yard where you belong.'

Poor bloody Hughenden. He was always being threatened with something. No wonder he tried to dump Ray whenever the opportunity arose. If Ray relaxed even slightly he was at risk.

The idle chatter continued until we came across a lone micky bull. Ray saw him before I did. He was grazing casually, probably thinking about good-looking heifers. We were downwind so he didn't scent us on the breeze. Ray looked at me with a smile and nodded. Nothing more was needed. We'd run him, then throw him, tie him and give him the full treatment – there and then, if we were successful. Off with the horns – Ray carried a little curved horn saw on his saddle; out with the nuts – a few seconds with the pocket knife would fix that; and earmarked in a second – I carried the marking pliers in my saddlebag. I'd also managed to stuff a couple of muesli bars in there too. Bloody Ray never stopped for smoko, and had bugger all apart from four cups of coffee for breakfast.

'What's he doing out here on his own?' I asked quietly.

'It's unusual.'

The micky wasn't too bad, for a scrubber – box-headed and beetle-arsed but carrying some beef. Possibly he'd copped a flogging for following his randy impulses and been put out of the mob by an older bull. If that was the case he would become a loner for a while until he developed a bit and the uncontrollable natural urges finally took over completely. Then he'd almost certainly rejoin the mob and skulk around the periphery for a while looking for a bit of stray sex while trying to avoid old Taurus. But the head lowering, snot snorting, horn waving and dirt pawing could only go on for so long – the showdown would have to come. He'd have to challenge the old boy formally – dart in and jab him in the guts with his spiky little horns. But if that didn't produce the desired effect, perhaps a quick rip up his old Khyber Pass would. That's if the micky could escape from us first.

However, if our induction ceremony was to be his destiny then most likely he'd settle right down and box up with the quiet cattle with no further thoughts of sowing his wild oats. We'd brand him the first time he was in the yards.

Ray pulled his battered high-crowned hat down tight and said, 'You ready? Let's go!'

I nodded.

His smile stretched ear to ear, 'Go at 'em from the jump.'

It was his favourite catchcry and he didn't have to be aboard a horse to utter it.

Ray barely touched Hughenden with the spurs yet the grey leapt to a gallop in a stride. Shit, he could go. He had lots of ability. So did Ray, who always carried a loose bull strap around his waist on the off-chance that something like this might happen.

Cheeky jumped a split second behind the grey and took off like a bullet as I grabbed for my hat. The brim flipped up and stayed there, à la Chad Morgan. If it had flipped down I would have been more like a headless chook, going somewhere but with no idea where. *This'll be fun*, I thought.

'I'll haze for you, Ray – up him!' I yelled, my heart belting hard, as the micky bolted through the scrub.

We ran the scrubber for two or three kilometres, Ray on the nearside and me hazing on the offside, keeping the animal as tight as we could between us. He was young and springy and could go like a greyhound as only young Brahmans can. Over washouts, up steep banks, over logs, under low scrub, we stayed with him. Ray was riding like a man possessed. The horses loved this as much as we did.

'He's nearly buggered. You ready?' I yelled.

'Yeah,' he answered, as he clamped the bull strap in his teeth and shifted his weight in the saddle.

The micky was starting to loop, an ungainly gait indicating rising exhaustion, and at any moment I expected Ray to lean down and grab him by the tail, pull him off balance and simultaneously dismount at the gallop, then throw him. I pushed Cheeky in close and waited for Ray to step off.

By now we were out on the edge of the mudflats where it was still dry, not far from where we'd come onto the lone micky in the first place. We'd nearly done a complete circle in the scrub. Then, without warning, the totally unexpected happened. The micky propped and took off at right angles behind my horse.

'Come around, ya dopey yang. It's not a bloody race,' I yelled, as I reefed Cheeky's head around. I think he was remembering his days on the track and he didn't want the race to end. It was probably the first time he'd ever been in front.

By the time I'd wheeled Cheeky, the agile little bastard of a micky had changed direction again, but Ray was still right on his tail. I hit Cheeky firmly with both spurs and if he'd jumped like that out of the barrier on the track he'd have been three lengths ahead in the first four. I think he even surprised himself. But then the same bloody thing happened, though this time the micky went under Cheeky and nearly had both of us spreadeagled on the mud-flat. Then he was in the water. We struggled to get to him and turn him, but he was heading straight for Chinaman Island and nothing was going to change his mind.

'After all that! If I had the rifle I'd shoot the bastard. Boundary fence, my arse,' Ray said.

At extremely low tides cattle often crossed over for a holiday on their bovine island resort, sometimes spending a few months there. They returned looking refreshed, usually when the water ran out, which was often at the same time as the good feed did. We should have guessed the micky's intention as he'd circled, but it hadn't crossed our minds.

We reined in and watched, disappointed, as he started to swim away. It was a rising tide and he'd have to swim most of the way – about four or five hundred metres. The horses weren't finished yet.

The chase had been exhilarating and they were blowing hard – but not as hard as Ray and I were. They were pulling on the bit and dancing, pouring sweat and flying foam, and were busting to continue. They'd run till they dropped when they were like this.

'Steady on, you bastard. Steady up, Hughenden.' Ray knew the best way to get the desired result was to dismount, so he did and the grey settled a bit.

The young Brahman was only about twenty or thirty metres out, maybe a bit more, just entering deep water when there was a sudden swirling disturbance and he disappeared from view. Momentarily his legs appeared, pointing skywards. It reminded me of a rickety table floating upside down. Then fleetingly he was upright and bellowing. Fins sliced the water, crisscrossing every which way, and the feeding frenzy created a blood boil. This was no crocodile, as had first flashed through my mind. How so many sharks were on the scene so quickly, and then gone just as quickly, was beyond me.

'Jesus Christ. What about that?' Ray said. 'It'd scare the saddle off a nightmare. Fuckin' hell. The poor bastard. Runs his guts out and gets eaten alive at the end of it.' We were speechless. A few moments later there was nothing but still water. A life had been snuffed out without trace in just twenty seconds. As we stood shaking our heads, a pair of sandpipers skimmed over the site barely thirty centimetres above the water. Life went on.

And to think we'd had crocodile phobia for the past few months after discovering slides in the mud. Neither of us had given a thought to sharks as we'd ridden over to explore Chinaman Island only a month ago. But the tides hadn't been as high as this, either there or back. We'd walked the horses over through water only fetlock deep an hour before dead low and returned within an hour of the turn. The disturbing incident gave us plenty of food for thought on the subdued ride back to camp.

The balance of Saturday turned into a bit of a non-event. Back in camp we hopped into a couple of sixpacks we'd brought with us. That seemed the right thing to do – a fitting end to the day.

Ray gave the camp oven plenty of attention during the early evening.

'Hey did I ever tell you about the time I invited the boss, the big boss, and his wife, and a few other business associates home for dinner one weekend? Real slickers they all were, but a great bunch. One bloke reckoned that all he knew about horses was that they had a head one end, a tail the other, and a leg on each corner. Anyway I'd promised them a real camp-oven meal. They didn't believe anyone really cooked like that. I'd been spruiking about how it would be something they'd remember for a while.'

I looked at him expectantly.

'Yeah, well it was. They'd never forget it all right. For a start I couldn't get the fire going. I'd dug a hole for a bed of coals and the bloody thing wouldn't go at all.'

'What, green wood?'

'No, when I dug the hole I didn't know I was right over the buried garden hose that ran under the lawn. I must have nicked it and caused a slight leak. When the fire got a bit of heat in it the nick must have got bigger and slowly the hole filled up with water. Thankfully that was just before the guests arrived so they didn't see the antics. But it made everything so late that I was in a bit of a rush.'

'So, what'd you do?' I asked, laughing. This was shaping up to be one of Ray's good stories, and he had plenty of them.

'Well it didn't take long to get on track with another fire. I stoked it up to a roaring blaze so it would come down to coals quickly. The guests all arrived not long after.'

'Yeah?'

'Finally I got the bloody roast on and had it sizzling and I settled down to have a beer with the boss, congratulating myself that I'd quickly got the situation under control. Anyway it wasn't much later that Robyn came over to the window and yelled out, "Ray, didn't you put any oil in with the roast? You'll burn the bum out of it."

'"Yeah, I put it in."

'"You couldn't have. It's not opened."

'"I used the other one."

'"What other one?"

'"The one on the sink."

'"Ray, what the hell have you used?"

'I looked over at the camp oven and couldn't believe my eyes. It had froth bubbling out of it. I'd used bloody dishwashing liquid in it.'

'Shit! No . . . What did you do?' This could only happen to Ray.

'Cooked them a steak on the barbie. I told them they were wallaby steaks I'd sliced off one I'd shot that morning. It took a while to convince them that it was really beef. One bloke wasn't real hungry,' he laughed.

So did I.

'Bit of an anticlimax,' Ray added, 'and I've had a lot of trouble living it down. The dog thought it was Christmas, though. The soap didn't seem to give him a guts ache either.'

'Well, what did you use tonight then?' I looked over to the galley and was relieved to see a bottle of cooking oil.

'No, I got this right. Once bitten, twice shy.'

The roast he turned out was delicious. Probably anything would have been delicious after six stubbies.

'Where *did* you learn to cook like that mate?'

'When I was ringing out west I was just a whippersnapper. We all had to take turns and I used to volunteer a lot because none of the others could cook at all.'

'Where were you ringing?'

'Out at Hughenden.'

'Does that explain something?'

'Guess so.'

'How long were you at it?'

'I was with Walsh's on and off for three years. They were contract musterers, cattle and sheep, as well as shearing contractors. I'd do the mustering season during the winter and come home to the surf club during the summer. I even did a bit of work in the sheds.'

'What? Shearing?'

'No, piece picking. Rousies they call them.'

'Why didn't you have a go at shearing?'

'I did, but it's a bit of a closed shop with the boss wanting to get the best value out of the shearers in the fastest time. Couldn't have novices wasting time – might have to feed the gang for an extra day. A lot of the owners are lousy bastards and treat shearers like vermin.'

'I've read a bit about that. Nothing much seems to have changed since the big strike, whenever that was.'

'Yeah. I was the only cattle ringer in the west who'd lie in his bunk reading *Surfing World*. My mates on the coast used to send it out to me. Winter beyond the black stump, summer this side of it. It was a pretty good lifestyle.'

Sunday morning was spent checking fencing and watering points then late in the afternoon we packed up and headed off. The horses had left the horse paddock to go down to the lagoon, so we closed the gate and locked them out to give the paddock a spell. We did this periodically as it was desirable to have a bit of feed there if they had to be confined overnight. We just managed to catch the ferry back to the mainland then set off on the long drive home.

It was always an anticlimax after a weekend and there was never much conversation, for a start anyway. Ray pushed the play button on the tape deck. 'A bit of old Slim is just the thing we need,' he said.

I preferred not to drive at night, and I trusted him completely. Relaxing was easy when the steering wheel was in his hands. He was a good safe highway driver and often preferred to tuck in behind a heavy transport, drop the lights to low beam and let the semitrailer clear the way ahead. Kangaroos were no match for the bullbar of a Kenworth. In addition, the communication network between the professional transport drivers pinpointed any radar traps – not a minor consideration. Lost in thought, I was jolted back to the present by the cassette clicking as it turned over to play the first side once again.

'Ray, I'm bloody sick of Slim. What else have you got?'

'Shit, don't say that. I don't want his image tarnished. "Leave him out there in the longyard do not rush him. Leave him out there with his mate the bally bay . . . " Shit, I've forgotten the next line.'

'I'll leave *you* out there in the longyard,' I threatened.

'Have a look in the glove box then. See what else is in there.'

I fiddled around and pulled out a couple more tapes, but I couldn't see the titles without putting the interior light on so I just slipped one into the deck.

'Where'd you get this crap? I think I prefer the fifth rendition of Slim's,' I said.

'That, my friend, is the Robert Cray Band. Don't you like the blues? No pleasing some people.'

The sound did grow on me a little. I might have even enjoyed it somewhat by the time it finished. 'You're a man for all seasons, Ray. A bit of a wildcard, you are.'

'I like to think of myself as a multi-faceted diamond,' he replied, glancing towards me with only the dash lights showing the faintest smile on his face.

'A rough diamond,' I said. 'Still needs cutting, I think.'

'I left myself wide open for that, didn't I?' he said and chuckled.

I saw Ray a week later, down at the pub. 'How'd you get on with the union, mate?'

'They want to take it further. But they're playing right into our hands. We'll let them take us to court, then we'll stall and if we lose we'll eventually lodge an appeal, dropping it on the courthouse steps if they agree to pay our costs. By the time that's sorted out the project will be finished.'

'You cunning buggers. More than one way to skin a cat, eh?'

'Yeah, you've got to go at 'em from the jump.'

'Where have I heard that before?'

On Friday night, a fortnight later, we repeated the long drive up the coastal highway, camping overnight as usual on the Boyne River. Early Saturday morning after a routine ferry crossing we were once again heading out from the little township to our bush camp. As we approached, everything looked normal – the gate to the horse paddock was still shut, and although we could see some vehicle tracks through the gateway, there was no cause for alarm. The tracks may even have been ours from the previous visit. Neither of us took that much notice. We could see three of our four horses making their way towards us.

'I wonder where old Hughenden is?' Ray squinted at the distant scrub in search of movement. 'He wouldn't leave the others.'

What we saw next appalled us. Teetering and tottering towards us was an apparition, a walking skeleton draped in raggy white, trying to neigh and threatening to topple over with every painful step.

'Whose horse is that?' I exclaimed. 'The poor bastard isn't long for this world. Where the hell could he have come from.'

'Jesus bloody Christ. It's poor old Hughenden!' Ray gasped as he recognised his best stockhorse. 'Shit, he's nearly done a perish. He must have been locked in here. I wonder if we accidentally locked him in when we left?' Tears sprang to his eyes.

'Would a horse last a fortnight without a drink?' I managed to ask, but couldn't trust myself to say more.

I didn't want to make eye contact with Ray. I turned away as he took his hat off and used one forearm then another to wipe his eyes.

'He couldn't have had a drink. There wasn't anything left in the waterhole. I checked it before we left – it was only mud.' Ray was already blaming himself.

Hughenden wanted to get past the ute that was half blocking the gateway. He was nearly dead on his feet, but seemed to have mustered a final spurt of energy.

'Don't let him through until we catch him. He'll do himself right in if he gets to the water. I've heard of this happening,' Ray yelled, his words snapping me out of my state of shock.

I slipped my belt off, looped it round Hughenden's neck and led him through. He tried to hurry, but he couldn't. Two hundred and fifty metres to the lagoon must have seemed like 10 kilometres to the completely dehydrated bag of bones. His eyes were so sunken it's a wonder he could see. Watching him stumble along was a pitiful sight. I was barely in control. Ray was following alongside in the ute and I could see he was still affected too.

'Don't let him drink too much when we get there,' Ray said. 'A bit at a time until he rehydrates, and not too fast.'

We needn't have worried. Hughenden's throat must have been so swollen that he couldn't swallow. He tried to drink, but all he could do was scoop up a bit of water then raise his head high enough to let it trickle down his parched throat. He stood for a long while, belly deep in the water, not moving, apart from his scooping action.

'A far cry from how he looked as a steward's horse at the race-track,' Ray said. 'We might as well go and get our chores done. He's not going to move for a while.'

We went up and unloaded our gear, chopped some firewood and had a bit of a look around.

'Hey, Ray, get a load of this,' I said as I went to fill the kettle, 'the poor bugger must have stood under the tank stand pawing the dirt for God knows how long. He would have been able to smell the water, but had no way of getting to it.'

The ground was always damp under the tap and he must have thought he could excavate a little pond.

'Come and we'll have a look at the dam,' Ray said.

The same evidence – mud all scraped away in search of mois-ture. And the tops of all the grasstrees had been eaten off down to the pithy flesh. They would have contained minute amounts of moisture.

We started to wonder how we could have locked him in. We were positive we'd seen all the horses go through the gate when we let them go.

Ray was trying to figure it out.

'Hughenden would have had to come back on his own before we left – in that period of about a quarter of an hour. But what for?'

'He'd hardly do that,' I said, shaking my head.

'He would have had to cover half a kilometre in total, there and back. I reckon he'd have had a drink and a bit of a feed then dozed off in the shade.'

'He wouldn't have left the others,' I insisted.

'If I find out one of those bastards from town locked him in I'll have him – properly. Mark my words.'

I had no doubt. I sure as hell wouldn't want to get in Ray's way. I'd never seen him violently angry, but this was his best horse. It might be different.

Going through all the possibilities on the way, we drove back down to the lagoon to check on the grey before doing anything else. He was still there and decidedly happier. But he wouldn't come out of the water. We called to him, and he gave that little snicker of acknowledgment that horses do and went in a little deeper. He was in up past his belly and we just sat and watched.

Ray and I turned in unison at the muffled sound of something padding along the deep dirt in the cattle track.

'Here come the others,' Ray said.

Cheeky, the blue horse, and old fleabite further back. Straight past they went, without a pause. They were obviously single-minded about their mission.

Uncharacteristically, instead of drinking, they all splashed right in, belly deep, to smell Hughenden.

'What's that all about?' I asked Ray.

'Beats me. Maybe they sense something is wrong and just wanted to check him out.' Then he added, 'Hey, do you know what I reckon has happened? I don't think we've caused this at all. I know a horse couldn't last fourteen days without water in this heat. I bet somebody has gone through and left the gate down because they were too bloody lazy to get out and shut it. Then they've shut it on their return a couple of hours later.'

'What, and Hughenden has come in while they were away?'

Ray nodded. 'Yep. You know how they come up to see if we're here and feed on the short couch grass around the camp. And I bet he was looking for a spray for sandflies – the poor bugger. That's what's happened all right. I'd stake my new saddle on it. We'd never be able to prove it though. Shit, I wish we didn't have that town lot to contend with. I'd like to bulldoze that end of the island right into the sea.'

'Yes, it's a pity we didn't take a bit more notice of those tracks. We've wiped them out now with ours over them.'

Ray was clearly shaken by all this, as I was. 'I don't know how much longer he'd have lasted. If he'd got off his feet he'd never have got up again. I'd say another half day at the outside.'

We both loved horses and although our lot had to work bloody hard and were never pampered, cruelty didn't have any place with either of us. We admired their ability and stamina without going overboard about it.

We spent a few hours on Saturday afternoon cutting timber and checked on Hughenden again when we returned. Nothing had changed. He was still in the water up to his belly. Maybe the slow drinking had saved his life.

'Geez, I hope he can get out,' I said.

'I'll go in and get him, I think,' Ray answered. 'He might need a bit of a gee up. If he bogs, he'll never pull himself out of it.'

But there was no trouble. He followed Ray onto the bank and immediately started to graze.

'Needed a bit of help to make up his mind whether or not the lagoon would still be there tomorrow,' Ray said, smiling now.

Just after daylight Sunday, when we checked again, he was running with the others – a completely different horse from the one we saw twenty hours before. It was a great sight. The rest of that day was filled with more timber cutting, then, after tying the gates open very securely to avoid a recurrence of Hughenden's near disaster, we headed off. It was about eleven o'clock when we neared home after the long drive.

I said to Ray, 'Ready to go back to the grindstone tomorrow mate?'

'No never, but it's a bit easier to take after a weekend like this. Not that we achieved much this trip.'

'Dunno. Saved a million-dollar horse. I bet *he* thinks we achieved something.'

'Yeah,' Ray answered. 'He means a bit to me – the rotten mongrel.'

He tacked the last bit on for my benefit, and glanced across towards me with a grin.

I smiled, then said to him, 'I've got to come into the city tomorrow. I haven't been there for years.'

'Well, come in to Waterfront Place. That's where I've been working. I'll meet you in the car park in the basement at 8.30. I've got to be back in court by 9.30,' he said.

'Okay, I'll do that.'

I met Ray right on time and got the shock of my life. I recognised his car, but I didn't recognise him at first and nearly walked straight past. He was wearing a classy-looking business suit and tie and carrying a smart briefcase.

'Jesus Christ, mate, I thought you worked for the company, not bloody owned it. All done up like a pox doctor's clerk. You'll be centrefold in *Cleo* next,' I said, but smiled to myself as I noticed he was wearing his R.M. Williams boots. Under the polished exterior the cowboy still lurked.

I had known for years that Ray was a glazier in the city. I also knew that the business he worked for had won the contract to supply and fit the glass in the Waterfront Place project. Ray had told me it was a substantial undertaking. I was about to find out just how substantial.

'Come around the front and I'll show you the foyer and then we'll go up in the lift.'

'Well I'll be buggered,' was all I could think of to say.

He nodded, matter-of-factly. The site had prime river frontage and the building was forty storeys, the tallest in Brisbane. The painters were putting some finishing touches to the entrance.

'Jesus, mate. What's your part in this?'

'I just do the glass bit.'

'What, all of it?'

He nodded.

'You mean you're the boss of the whole glass shebang, the whole shooting match?'

'I'm it. The buck stops here.' He nodded again.

'Mate, this would be a multimillion-dollar contract.'

'Multi *multi*.'

'Holy bloody hell!' I was completely blown away. Everywhere I looked there were huge panes of glass reaching high into the sky.

'Those painters remind me of an episode that happened a while ago with one of our blokes,' he said as we made our way up in the lift. 'It was on that building out at Lutwyche. You know, the one with those ugly green domes across the front.'

I nodded. I certainly did. Who couldn't notice it?

'Well, one of our glaziers had brought his ute in the tradies' entrance as they all had to do. He unloaded his glass from the A-frame and then thought he'd take a short cut via the front entrance – a lot of them did that when they thought I wasn't looking. There wasn't much overhead clearance, but they all knew it was just enough.'

'Hardly a problem, was it?' I asked.

'Normally not, but there were painters' trestles and planks set up right across the front of the building about four inches below the height of the entrance.'

'Oh, no. What happened?'

'Well, tearing the A-frame clean off the ute was very minor compared to the damage done to half a dozen Italian painters working along the scaffold. One plank went sideways and caught a couple of others on the way. That was just the beginning.'

'Bloody hell,' I said, imagining the scene.

'Pots of paint upside down on the footpath, unhappy painters upside down on the footpath, let alone the state of some of the pedestrians who were passing by.'

'What happened to the driver? No doubt they gave him some.'

'No, they didn't get a chance. He didn't stop or look back till he got back to the depot. By then every phone in the place was going off.'

'I bet.'

'Took a while to sort that mess out I can tell you,' he said and laughed. 'Well here we are,' he continued as the lift stopped with a slight jolt at the top floor of Waterfront Place, parts of it as yet without exterior glass. As I stepped out, vertigo got the better of me. I reeled back a bit. Somewhat recovered I inched forward and peered over the edge, hanging on for grim death.

'Shit, look at those blokes.' There were window cleaners several floors below.

'They go over the side in swinging stages – from the top here.'

'Bullshit. Is that right?'

'Yeah. They only work till the breeze gets up. It's pretty danger-ous, but they get the big money.'

'They'd need it.'

'They have to be half crazy to get the job, or half stoned to go over the side.'

I just shook my head. 'This is a whole other world. I don't know you at all, do I Ray?'

He just smiled.

KYLIE BRIAIS
Quiet achiever

—◦•◦—

'**B**lock up, Flash, block up!'
I could hear Dan's voice way up front but I couldn't see him. Then I caught a glimpse of a brown kelpie as the dog shot forward to steady the lead.

As the bullocks followed the cattle pads, every hoof kicked up a puff of smothering grey talc, adding to the dust cloud that travelled along with them. The tailenders were copping it, causing them to string out even further seeking the odd lungful of clean air. I was trying to keep the stragglers pushed up. There was no escaping the dust which hung low in the airless heat. Even drawing breath through clenched teeth, or slowly through the nose didn't improve things one bit.

Both Dan and I baked too, microwaved from the inside out, the internal furnace being fuelled with each intake of searing air.

My youngest son, Dan, and I were mustering for sale: three kelpies completed our team. Each trained dog was worth two men or more – a damn sight more responsive and reliable than many mounted ringers – and cheaper to feed by a country mile.

Old Flash, the trusted lead dog, along with Dan on his bike, had the educated Brahmans following dutifully. Any animals too eager were checked and steadied by Flash, who continually crisscrossed in front of their path. One, a more determined tearaway, was blocked and turned back with a severe bite to the nose. Bawling in surprise and pain it returned helter-skelter to the safety of the mob, with Flash dealing successive electric bites to its heels as part of its continuing rough education.

We rounded Rocky Knob and that meant we were six kilometres out from the homestead. I watched two of the dogs as they ranged up and down the wings, panting tongues of drool. They were fit and lean and worked like tigers. I felt proud to have bred them.

Back at the homestead my wife Karyn had taken the phone call. Before going into town she'd left a message on the kitchen table for me to read at lunchtime. It stated simply,

'Ring Kylie. She wants to talk to you about a job ad she found in *The Courier-Mail* this morning.'

Interesting, I mused. Our only daughter, Kylie, had become quite disheartened looking for work after she'd finished her studies. Jobs were hard to get. Her applications for about thirty positions as a graduate accountant had resulted in about a dozen interviews, but no job.

She'd completed her degree in accountancy at QUT and was one of only four or five offered a further placement there to do her honours year. However, after sixteen years of schooling she opted to join the workforce instead. More study could come later – probably her CPA, if circumstances allowed and if she could find a job. But there were many other graduates, similarly qualified, who were also out there looking for work – and against that competition she hadn't yet been lucky enough to land a position.

At one stage, she confided her doubts. 'Maybe I should do my honours . . . but I'm too late now for this year. I wonder if I could find something else to fill in till next semester?' Then, after a moment, she added, 'Dad, have you got a job for me?'

'As much as I'd like to say "yes", there's no job for you here. You know that. We're stretched keeping Dan fully employed. Don't despair. Something will come along soon.'

'Yeah, I know, Dad; it was just something to say. I didn't really mean it.'

She knew the situation on the land. Prices for fat beef cattle were good, but with the drought we didn't have many suitable for sale. The property was hardly big enough to support one family, let alone another worker as well. We'd probably look further afield for a bigger aggregation after a break in the weather.

Our family was totally immersed in things rural – always had been – and I had it in my mind that Kylie's lack of success to date might have been because she, too, was country through and through and it probably showed at her unsuccessful city interviews.

She'd only been applying for the metropolitan jobs because nothing more suitable had caught her eye. Maybe this attitude showed through too. It seemed that many positions were being filled before being properly advertised: perhaps as a result of some-body who knew somebody who knew somebody else. The slick city kids with contacts – the ones who walked the walk and talked the talk – were the types the finance companies and banks seemed to want. These youngsters brushed up well. They knew the ways of the metropolis and had no need to learn the commonsense ways of the bush.

I returned her call at lunchtime and her excitement was infectious.

'Dad, I've found the job I want. Do you know anything much about Stanbroke Pastoral Company? They want a trainee accountant.'

'Steady on a bit now. I can't listen that fast. Say it again?' I asked.

She read the whole advertisement to me and it certainly did sound like it was purpose-built for her. 'Rural experience preferred,' the last line stated. Good sign.

'Dad, do you know anything much about this company?' she asked, trying to keep herself in check, 'Are they the ones you were telling me about who fatten lots of bullocks in the Channel country?'

'Yes they are. They're huge – the biggest in Australia – and owned by AMP, which is totally Aussie too. Just don't put your application in yet. You'll need a different type of approach for this one.'

'What do you mean? What else do I need to say? The applications I've been putting in have seemed pretty good to me. I don't know how it's been going so wrong. Maybe my qualifications aren't good enough,' she said, momentarily doubting herself.

'Kylie, you nearly topped the course! Don't lose faith in yourself. Right now you need that more than ever.'

'I'm not, Dad. I'm just a bit disappointed about how hard it is to get a job.'

'Your rural experience will be the most important part of this application – don't sell yourself short on it. Make it your focus. You know a lot about the beef industry. Don't worry too much about your uni results – they're impressive on their own. And don't do anything till I get back to you. I'll jot down a few notes that might help you.'

After she hung up, I began listing Kylie's rural experience. Of course *she* knew what she'd done, but perhaps I could remind her of skills she'd forgotten she had. Included were: bookkeeping for our rural supplies business and grazing property; mustering, drafting and tailing out weaners; attending to water facilities, parasite control, pasture establishment and environmental issues; coordinating the barging of cattle on and off our island lease to coincide with suitable tides and mainland sales; cooking for a stock camp; yard building – the list went on and on.

When I rang back her mood had changed dramatically. She was crestfallen.

'Dad, I won't get that job against all the fellas,' she said quietly.

'Well you won't with an attitude like that,' I answered, a bit too sharply.

'But a lot of the males will have more experience than I have,' she continued.

'Not all-round experience like yours, though. Assume you will get it. Listen to this.'

Then I read out the list of her skills I'd prepared for her.

'Wow! Is that really me?' she laughed.

'Tell me the bits that aren't fact and I'll drop them,' I challenged.

She hesitated for a moment before answering. 'No, I suppose it's all true. I didn't know I'd done so much. But do you reckon I can put in an application like that?'

'If you want that job you can. You've got to stand out from the crowd. Believe me, they'll surely remember that girl with the 'wild west' experience. They will. They'll simply *have* to keep coming back to you. Your formal resume covers everything else. This will just be an exciting extra. I've got a hundred dollars to say the job is yours.'

She laughed, knowing full well that I was an incurable optimist.

Later she called back and said, 'Wish me luck. It's all done.'

Only a short time later she was called in for an interview. She rang me with the news, barely able to control her excitement. I told her I had expected nothing less. With an application like that I just knew she'd blitz the competition.

'Dad, this is only an interview. I've had a dozen of these and they've come to nothing.'

'Ye of little faith,' I said.

The interview was conducted by the company secretary. Kylie said afterwards that she quite liked his approachable manner. She thought he would be easy to work with because, among many other positive traits, he laughed readily. But her confidence drained when she was made aware of the number of applications they'd received for the position – some two hundred, and only a couple from women. Even so, she was happy enough with what had transpired – she couldn't do any better, she thought.

She hoped they would be impressed by her knowledge of the

company; that she had quizzed them as much as they quizzed her; that she had them listening as intently to her as she did to them; and that she appeared confident and well versed in all aspects of the beef industry.

Not long after that meeting another call from the company secretary informed her that she had been shortlisted and that they'd like to meet with her again as soon as possible. Then a couple of days later the same bloke unexpectedly rang me.

'Mr Winn, this is not usual practice, but since you sent in a reference for your daughter as her only previous employer, I'd like to talk to you a little about her. Do you mind if we follow this reference up a little?'

Mind, I thought to myself, just listen to me and I'll tell you about the smartest young girl I know – the one who is always cool and rational under any pressure and who always displays that all too rare trait called commonsense.

He asked a few questions about her academic achievements and then moved on to her rural experience. He was most interested in the family's island cattle interests. I got the idea that the secretary would have liked to have been there with us. Finally, he asked me if Kylie had any faults. I wondered what the hell he expected me to say about my only daughter who just happened to be the apple of my eye!

'No, she hasn't got any,' I answered truthfully.

So Kylie duly returned to answer whatever questions they had left for her. As it turned out, they didn't have much to ask her at all. When she was introduced to the managing director, he'd asked what her family hoped to achieve by cross-breeding cattle, which she'd mentioned in her original application. In particular, he was interested in the reason behind our decision to cross Limousin sires over Brahman dams.

'To put a rear end on a Brahman,' she'd answered honestly.

'That sounds a bit like something your father might say. Wouldn't it be better to say, "to beef up the hindquarters of the Brahman"?'

'I suppose that does sound a bit better. I'll tell Dad for future reference. But I'd already toned it down a bit. Dad's language is a fair bit stronger than that,' she'd said, smiling.

'I can just imagine. I started off as a ringer myself many years ago.'

Then he'd told her the job was hers!

Later that evening, as soon as she told the family the news, I went inside and came back with two fifty dollar notes. But she wouldn't accept them.

'No, Dad, you've done enough.'

And that was that. No argument. Did I say she was decisive, forceful, resolute? No? Well I should have.

Confident but apprehensive, calm but nervous, controlled but excited – that's how she seemed as she went off to work the following week to her first job.

Her smart city attire was a big change from her usual jeans, boots and hat. She left her dark hair to fall around her face instead of tying it in the usual quick and easy ponytail. Her capable hands, tanned and as usual bare of jewellery, complemented her fresh lightly made-up face.

Stanbroke head office had about twenty skilful and professional staff who managed the pastoral dynasty from a small but well-organised office in the Brisbane CBD.

The only hint of indulgence was that each staff office window framed a magnificent view of the Brisbane River with *Citycat* and the smaller *Kittycat* ferries plying back and forth; the stately *Kookaburra Queen*'s paddle wheels rhythmically slapping the water; jet skis zipping about defiantly, spouting thin plumes of water; and grammar school rowers with each stroke adding to the trailing wake of brief inline divots – an ever-changing panorama by day and an enchanting fairyland by night.

Behind Stanbroke's reception desk was a huge framed photographic print of another riverscape, though this one was viewed from horseback and vastly different. In the photo, 2000 head of fat Santa Gertrudis bullocks are swimming a flooded inland river – incongruously named Cooper Creek – which is formed by the confluence of the Thomson and the Barcoo rivers. The cattle had just been turned off Stanbroke's historic 7323 square kilometre Nappa Merrie station in the heart of the Channel country; home to the Burke and Wills 'dig tree' and close to the Queensland – South Australian border.

As the first professional female to be employed in head office, Kylie, and probably most of her colleagues, soon realised some social adjustments needed to be made. After all those rejections from city businesses she burst into this all-male territory with the confident resolve of having secured the right job for herself, but was soon brought down to earth with a thud. Kylie found herself in a kind of limbo, neither accepted within the female social group nor the male group. She was temporarily an outcast.

'Maybe I'm being paranoid,' she confided to Karyn and me. 'Maybe I'm taking things the wrong way and making too much of them.'

'Stay above it,' I replied.

'Just be yourself,' her mother added. 'They'll come round, you'll see.'

'Hello. Kylie Winn speaking. How can I help?'

'Who?'

'Kylie Winn. I'm the new trainee accountant. Who's calling please?'

No response.

'Hello, are you there?'

'Put me onto somebody who knows a bit about the place. Put me onto the boss,' the caller, a property manager, demanded impatiently.

And so she did – but she was bristling. *How rude*, she thought. *I wonder who he is, my first patronising chauvinist.* When Kylie told me about this call, I realised I'd been half-expecting this, but perhaps not so soon.

Kylie's measured response was noted silently by those in charge. Confrontation would have achieved nothing. However, in subsequent encounters the property manager continued to challenge her with his deplorable attitude. *I'll wear him down*, she decided. While maintaining good humour, some of it forced, and with some deference to him and his long service to the company, she set about it.

Things did improve a little as she focused interest on his work rather than on him. The Channel country became a favourite topic. He was passionate about it – a mine of information.

'Well, it's sort of bounded by the Diamantina River and Cooper Creek. It's the best natural fattening country in the world after rain, but rain that falls further north.

'It's one of only a few naturally irrigated areas in the world.

'The rivers run inland, down from the Barkly Tableland, and it can take as long as a month or even two for the waters to reach Birdsville. About twice a century big floods fill Lake Eyre.

'If there's a big monsoon up in the Gulf sometimes the rivers come down in a wall of water twenty or thirty feet deep.

'I've seen fat four-year-old bullocks turned off that country, and they've never seen a drop of water fall from the sky in their lives. The water all comes down the rivers and channels and spreads out for miles over the flat land.'

'He annoys me so much, Dad,' Kylie confided to me one evening after work.

'Sounds like the bastard knows what he's talking about, though, Kylie. He might just need a simple attitude adjustment,' I said, laughing and punching one closed fist into an open hand.

'Yeah, Dad, that would be the way, wouldn't it? Go into a new job and have your old man come into the office and deck one of the senior staff because the new junior was a wimp,' she responded, laughing too.

'You know, Kylie, there's one good way to handle buggers like that. Laugh at them. Don't ever let them think they've rattled you. Don't get angry, or if you do, don't let it show.'

'It's a hard ask that one, Dad.'

'Nothing deflates nastiness faster than turning it back on them lightheartedly, as if you think their lack of control is amusing, or it's had no effect on you.'

'I wouldn't be able to think of anything funny on the spur of the moment,' Kylie said.

'But you would if you'd thought about it beforehand and put it away in your mind or practised it a bit in imaginary conversations. You'll get to know his weak spots.'

She nodded.

'Everyone else within earshot usually laughs too, and after a second or two he'll have to as well to make out he wasn't serious. That gets them every time, if you can control your anger.'

'I can, Dad. You know how calculating I can be.'

'But I still reckon you'll need to practise. It's a bit of an art. I learnt that quickly when I first started going to court. Magistrates don't take kindly to anger. I nearly lost a case like that once in the Land Court, when I was just starting out.'

'Okay.'

'Yeah, take it on board, love, it works. It won't be long before he's your friend. Or he'll think he is. You're in control then, and he'll never know. Manipulate the bastard, like your mother does to me,' I laughed.

That Kylie was able to hold her own in the conference room, or anywhere else for that matter, and didn't crumble or take a backward step, might have impressed him a little. Having him admit it was another thing. But whatever the outcome, she was learning some of life's big lessons and her confidence was growing daily.

Stanbroke ran about 500 thousand head of cattle on thirty cattle properties spread across Queensland and the Northern Territory. The rangelands were chosen for their suitability for breeding, growing-out and fattening cattle and for their ability to assist with drought-proofing (cattle could be shifted from an affected area to another enjoying a more fortunate season). As part of her work, Kylie had to visit each of these properties on different occasions – commitments that were always welcome and exciting breaks for her.

On her first trip, I remember watching her disappear into the crowd at Brisbane airport. My heart had swelled with pride at the sight of the smart young girl dressed in jeans, Akubra hat and R.M. Williams boots – all worn for practical reasons rather than as personal statements.

'Dad, don't forget me – Thursday week, 10.30. Remember?' she'd said, smiling and then waving, her enthusiasm obvious in every movement and gesture.

After two or three connections with aircraft of ever-decreasing size, she finally landed on a dirt runway in the middle of nowhere. Some of the airstrips had a bough shed for shade, most had no toilet, and none had staff. For solitary visitors it could be a lonely wait for a final connection with a company aircraft. Kylie told me of an incident involving a new governess.

'Sorry about that,' the pilot had stated, but without sounding at all sorry or even perturbed. 'I hope you didn't mind waiting. I had to fly over to a neighbouring out-station and drop off their mail. It should have only taken an extra hour, but I had to pick up an Aboriginal boy who was seriously injured and fly as fast as this thing goes to connect with the Flying Doctor. I'm only three hours late – you're right aren't you? Get in quick. We'd better hurry. It's nearly dark and I don't have instrument rating.'

Not for the faint-hearted!

Regularly, Kylie was flown about in tiny company aircraft, visiting three or four properties per trip. It soon became routine – not quite mundane and never boring, but simply accepted as part of the job. However, there was one trip that she would never forget.

The single-engine, four-seater Cessna was ready for take-off from Charleville bound for Bulloo Downs, near the Queensland – New South Wales border. The pilot had listened to the weather report as it crackled from the radio.

'Isolated storms over . . . Warrego . . . the south-west . . . wind . . . knots . . .'

'Is everything all right?' Kylie asked, 'I've never been in such a small plane.'

'Yeah, it'll be okay. I think they mean storms closer in. We're heading south-west. We should skirt them. Probably won't see a trace of any activity.' And so the Cessna took to the sky with one other passenger aboard.

The storms hit without warning – literally out of the blue. The Cessna had been flying south-west as fast as it could but the storms were travelling east at an alarming pace. In only a minute or two, the plane was consumed by the rolling blackness of a violent electrical disturbance. Buffeted and battered, it would climb a hundred feet, then drop two hundred. Kylie's rucksack hit the roof then slumped to the floor and slid sideways under her seat before she could grab it.

'Secure anything loose before somebody is knocked uncon-
scious,' the pilot yelled, but he was barely audible, despite being
less than two metres away.

Concentrating intently, he juggled the controls. Snaking flashes
of blinding white light alternated with exploding ink-black darkness. Kylie said she and the other passenger were close to panic,
but not the pilot. He was stoic, collected – his eyes fixed on rows
of dials, flying wild and trusting instruments alone.

'Hang on,' he yelled as he dropped the Cessna into a steep
dive.

A free-fall! Their hearts were in their mouths – sudden weight-
lessness and disorientation. This was it . . .

'We'll have to see it out,' the pilot shouted. 'Tighten your seat-
belts. The worst might still be in front of us.'

His determined expression didn't allay any fears.

'Stay with me. I've got to go down further. Hopefully we'll come
under it. I've still got a bit of altitude. Don't panic.'

Suddenly the pilot pulled the plane out of the dive and levelled
into blinding sunlight. Day dawned in an instant.

'Jesus H. Christ!' the other passenger gasped, relieved. A little
colour had started to return to his cheeks.

'Don't take his name in vain for God's sake – he was the bastard
who saved us,' the pilot chuckled, shaking his head.

Kylie checked her watch. It had felt like they'd been captive
in the storm for half an hour, but she worked out it was only a few
minutes.

'Does this happen very often?' she asked the pilot.

'Not as wild as that. I'll have to divert to Cunnamulla. There's bound to be a line of those storms – always is. I don't want another dose just yet. And I want to check out my little mate here. She's copped a bit of a gruelling.'

He was beaming, obviously relieved, but with adrenalin still pumping. He sat looking pleased with himself as he radioed ahead, and an hour later they touched down at Cunnamulla. Kylie told me it had crossed her mind that everybody there should have been pleased to see them alive, but not a soul raised an eyebrow. In fact there was not a soul at the airport to raise an eyebrow.

They explored Cunnamulla – it took five minutes – and then retired to the hotel for the night.

As the first grey light of breaking dawn crystallised into brilliant freshness, they swung south to Bulloo Downs.

Kylie had a story to tell that night around the barbecue. The managing director and a couple of other office staff had preceded her by twenty-four hours, returning from the property inspection that Kylie had missed.

All of the property staff turned up for the barbecue: the visiting group manager (who managed four properties); the pilot (who doubled as a gardener or an extra hand in the yards when not in the air); the overseer (who was the boss in the manager's absence); the head stockman (in charge of the full stock camp comprising three ringers – two of them seasonally employed Aborigines – and four jackaroos at various stages of their training); the contract horse breaker (employed yearly to educate the weanlings); the bore runner (who carried out regular bore inspections); the mechanic (who serviced the four properties); the governess (who looked after the children and supervised their School of the Air lessons); and the two cooks (one each for the musterers' camp and homestead) plus their wives, husbands, children and dogs. It was one of their rare social occasions, and they made the most of it.

During the evening, many recounted bad flying experiences that progressed from probable to improbable to impossible. It was only when Kylie's pilot started on some of his own escapades that the earlier stories paled into insignificance. The exaggeration seemed to be in direct proportion to the amount of scotch and rum consumed.

Dawn saw all hands on deck – in body at least. The jackeroos, who'd not been permitted to imbibe the night before, had obviously been schooled to turn out early on their horses to pose for a photo for the staff magazine. They looked decidedly fresh – impressing the big boss was paramount. A lot of the other staff turned up too, some for various photos and others as onlookers.

'Want to hear a funny story, Dad?' Kylie asked me later when we were discussing this first trip.

I nodded.

'When we were all out in front of the homestead and the jackeroos had to pose for the photos, one of the new boys had a bit of trouble in the clothing department. He's fairly fat, and that was the trouble.'

'Yeah, you told me about him. Nice kid. You interviewed him didn't you?'

'Sort of. Anyway he'd made a serious misjudgement. His new jeans were simply too tight for him. Maybe he'd planned to lose a bit of weight, but the cook was too good.'

She grinned. 'Obviously he'd struggled and eventually succeeded in getting them on, but then there was another problem. He couldn't lift his leg high enough to get on his horse.'

'Poor bugger, and in front of the big boss too.'

'What made it worse was when somebody yelled out "if you stand on your head your foot might reach the stirrup".'

'The bastard . . . What happened?'

'After three or four goes he got redder and redder until he eventually had to accept a leg-up.'

'I hope his mates didn't go too hard on him.'

'He'll probably get a lot worse than that, Dad,' said Kylie.

The head office staff visit had been planned to coincide with a local campdraft – 'local' being a mere two hundred and thirty kilometres away – and the very subdued party set off. Campdrafting is the favourite sport of most rural people in the beef industry, whether male or female, young or old, and entails pitting the skill of a horse and its rider against a beast through a prescribed course. At every opportunity, staff from most neighbouring properties turn up to compete.

The meeting also included a broncoing contest. This involves lassoing a beast from a mob and skull-dragging it, using a heavy horse, to a panel of rails in the middle of the stockyard. Once it is secured against the rails, the stockmen throw the animal and give it various treatments including dehorning, castration, branding, earmarking, various inoculations and bangtailing (cutting the hairy brush of the tail square for easy identification). Kylie said that there were no partygoers that night, which wasn't surprising given a 460-kilometre round trip and a full day of horse and cattle sports.

The next day's itinerary was dominated by property inspections in the Toyota Landcruiser. On the way back to the homestead via the 'goat track' a couple of middle-aged property staff jokingly offered Kylie the wheel of the four-wheel drive. To their surprise she took it.

'You would have loved it, Dad,' Kylie said as she related the incident to me. 'They thought I couldn't drive, being an accountant and working in the city.'

'Bad mistake.'

'It was absolutely hilarious,' she laughed. 'One of them said, "Steady, Kylie. These things roll over pretty easily".'

'What did you tell him?'

'"Nah, they're pretty stable really. They'll slide before they roll." You should have seen the look on his face. He and the other bloke were *packing* it. So I put my foot down properly then.'

'Serves them right.'

'I said to them, "You should see Dad running up the fresh horses some mornings. He roars up and slides in beside the mob to send them in through the gate if they look like they're going to veer off".'

'What did they say?'

'Not much. I told them that Cruisers were better than Nissans – they slide more easily and that we'd rolled a couple of Nissans but never a Cruiser.'

'Wish I'd been there.'

'Yeah. Things went a bit quiet for a while.'

Apparently, by the time they returned, the passengers were white-knuckled and speechless. She taught them a thing or two about real four-wheel driving – and hopefully, about chauvinism. News of the episode spread like wildfire throughout the company properties and some grudging respect may have been earned – though there's no way of telling. Or maybe there is as she was never offered the wheel again.

I collected her on Thursday at 10.30 as promised. The late-night crowd at Brisbane airport barely gave a second glance to the just wakened girl with the dusty, crumpled Akubra and the creased chambré shirt bearing the embroidered name Stanbroke Pastoral Company.

'Dad, I've had the best week,' she said, 'I've got the greatest job.'

Ten years later I met Kylie at the Brisbane Royal Show. It was always a big week for her, but she was an old hand. During the first couple of days, as usual, many of the Stanbroke staff had gathered at the Brahman judging: managers, overseers, the CEO and the company secretary, ringers and jackaroos, the new female vet and Kylie, the company accountant.

She asked, 'Dad, do you remember my boss, Terry Williams?'

'G'day, mate. Course I remember. We talked half the night at your wedding, Kylie.'

We shook hands. 'Good to see you again, Terry.'

We swapped pleasantries before he asked, 'Remember when I called you to ask about Kylie before she started with Stanbroke —'

I cut him off, 'Yeah, and I told you a pack of lies.'

'Well, I was going to say thanks,' he half-smiled at my joke. 'She has added a lot to the company.'

'Geez, Kylie, you can wear your halo as a hatband.'

'Kylie has been part of a pretty exciting period in Stanbroke. She paved the way for other female staff. I realise it was hard for her at the start.'

Kylie answered, 'No, it wasn't that bad.'

'It's a good team, Rhylle. No one stands above the others, except the CEO,' said Terry with a grin. 'Kylie, don't look now but your original retrained chauvinist is heading this way.'

The property manager smiled as he approached. 'Kylie, I've been looking for you. Do you know offhand what the throughput was at the feedlot last year?' Then he turned to Terry and continued, 'She's the only one around here who knows anything.'

GEORGE WILSON
Island cattleman

———•◆•———

I peered around the doorway of room No. 13 of the general ward
at Gladstone hospital and wondered if George's room alloca-
tion had been left to somebody whose sense of humour was a bit
off-centre. As I'd progressed along the passageway I'd noticed that
every other room seemed to be unoccupied. Any of these would
have been better than 13. But George was a fairly serious sort of
bloke anyway, so I doubted superstition was part of his make-up.

'George. How'yer goin', mate? Bastard of a way to finish up.'

'Yeah, but I'll be right. Give us a month and I'll be back in the
saddle.'

My heart skipped a beat. They mustn't have told him yet.
I knew I had to be careful about what I said.

'You reckon?'

'Yeah, I'll have to be. I've got those weaners to cross with the
low tides next month.'

'Can't keep a good man down.'

'Dunno about a good man, but those weaners won't swim themselves out, will they.'

It was so different seeing George like this. It was as if he'd been stripped of his identity. His glasses – prescription ones that darken in sunlight – sat on his bedside table. I'd rarely seen him without a hat and the lack of grey in his hair surprised me. His tanned face was paler than usual, or maybe it was just the fluoros. It wouldn't have seemed out of place for him to sit up and light his pipe – not for me anyway, but maybe for the nurses.

I stayed a while, but he looked so tired I cut it short. As I prepared to leave I noticed the board above his bed. I was surprised I hadn't seen it earlier. Written there was the instruction, 'Nil by mouth' and underneath, 'Chris Wilson'.

'Bloody hell, George. How long has your name been Chris?'

'Since I was born. You don't have to tell the world, do you?'

'No bloody wonder the air ambulance couldn't find you on their list.'

'Yeah, useless bastards,' he smiled weakly.

George was the boss of Monte Cristo, 87 000 acres of Curtis Island cattle country off the Central Queensland coast. It was literally *just* off the coast, separated from it here and there by about three-hundred metres of treacherous waters – at low tide that is. At high tide it was a different story because rising waters broadened that span to nearly a kilometre. Just a thoroughbred sprint from the homestead, the island almost touched the mainland at a place called Ramsay's Crossing, the narrowest part of the strait known simply and not very imaginatively as The Narrows.

Varying in exact location due to the vagaries of the tides, up to five metres at times, but always south of the Crossing, was a no-man's land – or more accurately a 'no-man's water'. The tide at Gladstone, 60 kilometres to the south, turned an hour earlier than that at Rockhampton, 60 kilometres to the north. Consequently, the northbound tidal inflow surged mightily up the narrow strait, with no resistance from the last of the retreating tide at Rocky. Not long after the turn, similar forces, but in reverse, sent fast waters down from the north. Twice daily the confused collision of water created baffling conditions.

Yachties used this shortcut – the judgment of some at times clouded by suicidal bravado. For safe passage they had to identify the small window of opportunity created by the combination of enough water below and not too much on top. That was the test. Some failed.

But the fishing and crabbing were superb, par excellence, and many an amateur skipper and not just a few professionals had become highly skilled in the quest.

George sent the Monte Cristo cattle turn-off to the mainland under these conditions. Almost single-handedly, except for his capable wife, Joy, and casual staff hired for peak periods of mustering and crossing cattle a couple of weeks a year, he managed the two or three thousand-head cattle breeding enterprise for Tim Regal, a New York stockbroker, and his father.

Apart from Monte Cristo and the tiny settlement of Southend there were two other grazing properties on the island. A couple of years earlier I had taken over a twenty thousand-acre lease on one of them (with a partner, Ray), working it part-time on most weekends. And so we became George's neighbour. We'd thought there'd be a romance about island life, but instead we found a bloody lot of unforseen problems.

George was promoted from ringer to manager of Monte (his term of endearment), at the age of just twenty-two. This was most unusual, and happened by accident. The homestead burnt down – and the manager at the time had nowhere to live with his family. George had somewhere to live – in his swag – and nobody else wanted the job. He'd been brought up on the Queensland and northern New South Wales stock routes and that gave him twenty-two years more experience than most managers. Thirty-five years later he was still there. A quiet, capable man, he had faced many tough situations during his years on the island. Seeing him lying there on his hospital bed, I wondered if his greatest challenge was yet to come.

After telling George I'd see him later, and checking with Joy to see if there was anything else I could do to help, I headed for home base, a little town named Dayboro, about forty kilometres north-west of Brisbane. On my way back, I thought about a time when we were first on the island. There was a big mob to cross, with George in charge. Swimming cattle off an island sounds grand. It's also highly dangerous: hard on the cattle, the swimming horses, the dogs and the men. Not for the faint-hearted.

Dutifully, but under simmering protest, George had mustered and drafted 400 half-educated weaners. The New York stockbrokers were having a lean time of it and the word had come through, 'Sell weaners quickly!'

George had replied, 'They're not ready for another month. I haven't finished teaching them their manners yet.'

But the call was insistent, 'Sell weaners quickly!'

'There's no low water for another month. It's too dangerous,' argued George.

'Sell weaners quickly!'

And that was that. George needed his job and the brokers were the bosses.

The little Brahmans were good types and would sell well. Monte Cristo's twice-yearly turn-off always created stiff competition. Even though they were well grown, the island country wouldn't fatten them. Repeat buyers knew full well how the cattle bloomed when pastured on softer mainland country. But this lot were still half-wild and they were nowhere near ready for the saleyards. Cattle marketed without having had any work done with them reflected on the man in charge. It made George wild to think about it. It was *his* reputation that would be damaged.

The bewildered babies were yarded at The Narrows to await the only possible tide, still a metre above the desirable low that would have occurred by the time they were fully educated. Even when conditions were optimum there was often trouble with these crossings. George was always on edge about this part of his job, but insisted that the rest made up for it.

As we arrived, a mate named Kevin and I looked at each other, then Kevin turned to George. 'Shit, these weaners are just off their mothers.'

'I know, mate, but I just do what I'm told.'

I said, 'There's plenty of water. When's low tide?'

'This is it,' George said, 'another quarter of an hour and it'll be as low as it's going to get.'

'Fuckin' hell, George, they'll have to swim half a bloody mile,' Kevin said, trying to estimate the distance across the water – always a hard thing to do.

George was furious. 'It's no bloody joke, is it. One day there'll be a serious accident attempting fool things like this.'

I said, 'I wonder what the Workplace Health and Safety blokes would say about it.'

'A bloody lot,' George answered, 'and I've got these blokes to answer for too,' he said, indicating a couple of other ringers nearby making adjustments to their gear for the swim. 'Come and meet them.'

We walked over and as we did, old 'Cyclone', George's mate and nearly eighty years old, entered the water from the mainland on horseback. From where we were he was just a speck in the distance and I didn't know how George could see him.

'How'd he get the nickname "Cyclone"?' I asked George.

'It's not his nickname mate. It's his real name. His mother named him that because he was born in a cyclone.'

'Bullshit.'

'Yeah, it *is* bullshit. No, he could cut through the bush like a cyclone. Ride like the wind. Still can, only it's down to a bit of a breeze. He was a jockey when he was younger.'

'Getting a bit old for this sort of thing, isn't he?' I suggested.

'Tell *him* that,' replied George. 'We couldn't do without him. He's been doing this for forty years. He'd die if he stopped. Geez it was funny there a while back.'

We both looked towards him expectantly.

'We called into the Mt Larcom pub for a drink before I came over home in the dinghy. He bowls up to the bar and yells out, "There was only ever three tough men in Queensland and the other two are dead. Give me a rum, fast." You know what the barman said? "Piss off, Cyc, you look like you've had enough already." Geez it was funny. He's a bloody larrikin, the old boy. Do you know what he told me on the phone the other night when I rang to see if he would help, and asked him to bring his dogs? He reckoned he'd been helping muster a rough paddock down south of here last week and the scrub was so thick his dogs had to wag their tails up and down instead of sideways. Christ he's a doer.'

After what seemed an eternity, where his horse alternately swam then struggled to walk in the shallower spots, Cyclone beached right on the ramp and waited till his dogs caught up. We could see there was nearly no run in the tide either way, indicating dead low. Then he greeted us all.

'These bloody Yanks got shit for brains!' he said loudly to no one in particular. Being deaf, his volume always seemed to be turned up a couple of notches. 'Somebody'll get drowned here if those bastards don't wake up to themselves.'

We all looked at one another then nodded to Cyclone.

'We were just saying the same thing, mate. Come on, push those old pensioners in before I change my mind about the whole bloody thing,' George yelled to be heard. He was getting more and more tense. He didn't like this one bit.

Cyclone followed the normal practice and entered the water first. His job was to lead the cattle out. Following him half a dozen old pensioner station horses splashed in. They knew their job – they'd spent all their working lives making the crossings, behind the mob for most of it rather than in front. As they entered, a couple of them looked back to see if the cattle were following. Cyclone's dogs stayed back and helped George's dogs with the unruly mob now being pushed down the ramp and into the sea.

'Righto fellas, send 'em in, keep right on 'em, and give 'em plenty of whip or they'll start ringing in the water and double back. If they do and you can't turn 'em, get out of the bloody way or they'll drown you and your horse,' then as an afterthought he added, 'and probably a few dozen of themselves. You blokes on the wings, keep 'em straight.' George seemed better now that we'd started. The waiting was the worst.

The cattle were apprehensive, baulking at descending the ramp. The poor little poddies hadn't been educated enough to follow the old horses. All tropical breeds, being of the *Bos indicus* species, do have that trait as a natural tendency, but it has to be developed. To date, this small consignment had only been 'tailed out' – released from the yards under tight control for short periods and then returned for the night – and taught to stand and 'face up' to an approaching horseman. But with the lead Brahmans about fifty metres out in the water, swimming straight like little troopers, all looked well. Too easy, I thought, Christ this is a buzz. Then, just as I started to relax a little, the ones in front decided to veer off, perhaps because they thought they were getting too far away from home.

'Give 'em plenty of whip! Get up 'em! Push 'em back straight. Make that bloody horse swim instead of feeling for the bottom, Rhylle. He knows what he should be doing. Give him the double of the whip, the lazy old bastard, and push 'em up,' George yelled. 'You blokes on the wings, get in closer and straighten 'em,' he bellowed even louder.

But with the noise created by the splashing of sixteen hundred and twenty swimming legs, more if you count the dogs, his voice was nearly lost on all but those closest, so each ringer just did the best that his training and experience dictated.

'Look out! Look out! They're going the other way. Get in on 'em. Push 'em over. Christ, there'll be an accident here in a minute!'

We were all trying to listen to George through the noise, but only the odd word was audible. For a moment we thought we had them, but then they swung right around the other way, completely off the shallower crossing, and entered treacherous deep water.

'Get out of the way! Get clear of 'em!'

The complete mob was ringing and the only thing to do now was save ourselves. The little Brahmans were trying to clamber up on the horses.

'They're coming back – *get out of the way or they'll drown you!*'

We heard every word this time.

Panic-stricken, desperately feeling for something solid underfoot, the babies tried to climb up on each other's backs, but only succeeded in pushing their mates under. The victims surfaced a metre away and after the ducking tried even harder to do the same to others close by.

Our saddle horses were now swimming hard, but the old pensioners ploughed on ahead, probably oblivious to the mayhem behind them. Cyclone turned them back. I imagined them thinking, what's this bloody old fool doing – we're nowhere near over.

'Get off and give your horse a chance. *Grab him by the tail!*' George bellowed. It was reassuring having this experienced stockman so close. He was in control, even if the situation wasn't. I would have done whatever he said. Feeling the horse tiring beneath me I slid backwards out of the saddle, hanging onto the long reins with my teeth. After I grabbed his tail securely, I spat the now stretched reins out. The poor bugger didn't need my weight pushing him under. If I'd missed the tail it would have been the end of me because I'm pretty hopeless in the water. Luckily the horses were all used to long swims. Then a thought shot through my brain like a lightning bolt. I suppose all the crook swimmers were shark tucker long ago. But you'd have to be dead unlucky to be the one out of four hundred to be taken. *Dead* unlucky all right. I told myself to stay in control – for Christ's sake don't panic!

As my horse returned to shallower water I knew to let go of his tail before he discovered what he'd been towing and gave me a double-barrelled kick in the guts. But I also knew that if I let go too soon I'd still be in trouble in deep water. I had to get it right or else!

We were first out of the water because I'd been bringing up the tail, in more ways than one, the easiest job and safest for novices. When the mob turned it put me in the lead so I remounted quickly as the mob followed, crowding up the fifty- or sixty-foot wide gravel ramp. The mob bulged at the entrance forcing some to peel off the flank and struggle up the steep muddy banks on either side of the ramp. Others inadvertently followed them, but didn't go far in the waist-deep mud.

There was no way of knowing, yet, if any cattle had drowned, although twenty-seven were bogged. Two dogs were missing. We presumed they'd drowned – the poor buggers dying in the line of duty.

'Bloody lucky nobody went under,' George said as he glanced around. 'That's only the second time that's ever happened, and for the same reason. Never again! They can jam their job if they ever ask me to do this again, before cattle are educated.'

'Sorry we weren't more help, mate,' I said to George.

'Don't blame yourself or anyone, ever. It wasn't anybody's fault who's in Australia.'

We got the message.

It was already too late to try again that tide. Subsequent attempts would almost certainly have had the same result while the recent experience was still fresh in the animals' minds. The quickening tidal flow reinforced the decision. In any case, we couldn't leave those exhausted little ones bogged. They'd all given up the futile struggle. Resigning themselves to whatever awaited them they stood (or sort of floated) quietly, shoulder deep in the gluey mire. It was impossible to walk upright to them. The first step you took off the ramp proved that.

'You'll have to get on your gutses and wriggle around – like this,' George demonstrated.

So we took off our shirts and boots and slid around on our bellies trying to pull the heads of the bogged weaners uphill, so that the incoming tide wouldn't drown them before it set them free. George assured us that the high tide would float them out soon enough. It was a 4-metre tide that evening, not as big as they get, but certainly high enough to put the animals at least 2 metres underwater if they didn't rise out of the mud.

I was sceptical, convinced they'd all drown. However, I didn't dwell on it and did as George asked, going from one to the other and wrestling them around uphill. Close proximity to man caused a renewed struggle and we took advantage of that to make the turning easier. Some had struggled away a good distance and I was surprised how easy it was to wriggle to them horizontally, it felt like swimming across an acre of axle grease.

We'd just finished the last one and were having a bit of a breather before sliding back to the ramp when George called, 'Don't waste any time, you blokes, I saw a bloody big crocodile in there about this time last year.'

'Did you? Bullshit!'

'Bloody oath I did.'

What happened next will live in my memory forever. We slid across the mud on our gutses, looking like we were propelled by outboards on our feet and paddlewheels on each shoulder. No crocodile alive could have come within a bull's roar of any of us.

'Why the bloody hell didn't you tell us before?' we demanded.

'Then I wouldn't have had any helpers, would I?' George finally said, after he'd recovered from his idea of humour.

It was a big job getting clean and we were all a bit windy about getting back in the water. So we called at a dam on the way back to the homestead and did a proper job of it – with no threat of underwater company.

Next morning the weaners that had been bogged were huddled outside the gate beside their mates who were still penned from the day before. Every one of them was there, just as George said they would be. And how good was it to see the two missing dogs, standing guard over the errant twenty-seven? The cattle were washed clean, but the poor dogs were still caked in mud and barely recognisable. They were hungry and very happy to see us. They knew nothing else other than work, and would have waited there a week if need be. Not a pallet of Pal, or a ute-load of Meaty-bites, or for that matter a hunk of scrub bull's bum, which was more likely, would have distracted the dogs from their job.

On day two, Plan B was activated. We were going to try again to cross the cattle, with basically the same plan and one slight variation. To execute the idea we'd either have to work at high tide, or during the night at low tide. The dark didn't appeal even though high tide meant working underwater for some of the time. It was a challenge. We were going to pin together as many portable fence panels as possible to extend the race, the sides of which ran down either side of the gravel ramp into the water, hoping it might give more direction to the mob. When the tide dropped we would be mounted and ready for a crossing. By then the tops of the panels would be above the water and keep the mob straight, for a start anyway. It meant twitching or pinning the panels together underwater and 'Cobb and Co-ing' with heavy wire – the first panel to the heavy post at the end of the race on either side. We all stripped off and worked as best we could between regular resurfacings.

Eventually we finished, and as we all stood about naked and muddy somebody said, 'That's what I call experiencing life in the raw!' The moment passed very quickly as Joy arrived in her little Suzuki four-wheel drive with lunch for all, and a movie camera.

Finally, low tide came. We were so well prepared as we repeated the previous day's exercise that it was a bit of an anticlimax, though probably not for George. We sent a bigger mob of horses in front, behind Cyclone, and kept the weaners right in their wake. In fact, some of them swam out in front, and as they paddled along, the horses kept the lead straight. It was a big swim, but everything worked like clockwork. The mob behaved like old hands.

After landing, the lead horses were cut out and turned back. The ringers took the mob on to the yards a mile or two up the road. They were no trouble now. Later in the afternoon the transports would load and deliver them to Gracemere Saleyards at Rockhampton, only an hour away.

We turned and prepared to repeat our swim in the other direction.

'Will we push these old pensioners back in front of us, George?' I asked.

'No, leave them. They'll come back when they're ready – maybe the next low tide or the next or the next. It's like a holiday for them. They like it over here until they discover they're on their own.'

I was taken with George's confidence in, and his consideration for these retired workers. It was easy to see he loved them all. But even though they'd retired from active stock work they still played an important part in each crossing. It was heart-warming to witness.

Already there was a strong run in the tide as it was now well past the turn. The station dogs looked like they would have the worst of it on the return journey. However, at George's suggestion we each tied our whip to a dog's collar and towed him across, like a little dingy bobbing in the wake of a ferry. Then I noticed that George hadn't followed suit. I was puzzled that he hadn't obeyed his own instruction, but the riddle was soon solved. One dog wouldn't have a bar of the whip and instead grabbed a mouthful of George's horse's tail and hitched a ride.

When I spotted the dog, I looked around to tell George, but before I could say anything he spoke, smiling. 'He always was an independent bastard, that old fella. He gets a few kicks, but he still must reckon it's worth it. He might be whip shy but he's no fool.' George was proud of him, and who wouldn't be?

We were all happy and relieved at the success of our second attempt. There were some good stories that night – they got better and better as the night wore on.

Day three saw us stripped off again and just entering the water to retrieve the panels, once again with plenty of water about, when George bellowed urgently from the ramp, 'Don't move, anybody. Look out in front of you!'

We all looked . . . and looked. I was peering right over to the mainland expecting to see old Cyclone coming across again, or something.

'What are we looking at, George?' one of the ringers asked.

'That's no log in front of you. It's going against the current. Come out quickly and no splashing about.'

Now there was a bloody contradiction if ever there was one.

By the time we spotted the big saltwater crocodile, George had grabbed the rifle from his Cruiser. My blood ran cold as I watched the croc slowly gliding towards the spot we'd just vacated – one of us would almost certainly have been taken but for George's vigilance.

BOOM! The bullet didn't kick up a spurt of water so I guessed it had hit something solid.

'Good shot, mate,' I said.

'Nah, just scared him. The bastards are protected,' George replied.

'Dunno, George. I reckon you hit him.' Kevin was adamant.

'He'd have dived, mate.' George turned away, preparing to slide the rifle into the cover that was strapped to the dashboard of the Cruiser, but then changed his mind and propped it up against a post instead.

Kev turned to me with a half grin. 'Ask no questions and be told no lies.'

We undid the panels from the posts at the end of the wooden race and dragged each section – still linked together – out of the water with the Cruiser. We unpinned them there on the gravel ramp. George sat high on a post cradling his rifle and scanning the water, perhaps thinking of the joke he'd played on us the day before when we were in the mud, and to which he'd owned up that night – there hadn't been a croc there twelve months ago at all.

The croc sighting had changed the mood, and we were all quiet as we worked.

'Must have been the regularity of our being here at the same time each day. I wonder if they're that smart,' George said, clearly still a little concerned. He was the boss, responsible for all five of us, and now that responsibility had been tested, it weighed heavily on him.

'I didn't know the bloody things came this far south, George,' Kevin said.

'They bloody never used to until they protected the bastards. Now they're expanding the boundaries of their traditional territory.

Not long ago a girl in a canoe in the Fitzroy River had her paddle bitten in half. Somebody will be taken soon,' he said.

'Do you reckon that one will be back?' somebody asked.

'Nah, I think he would've dived pretty deep, don't you?' And George turned away, winking at me.

As I continued driving home from the hospital, I wondered if George really thought he'd be okay to muster in a month's time. He was in a fairly bad way, but I'd found out long ago that he was as tough as old boots.

While my mate Ray and I were taking up our tenancy his help had been invaluable. On the odd occasion that we hadn't taken his advice, well, we invariably ended up with egg on our faces. But he never said, 'I told you so'. Instead he'd recount one of his own stories of failure and the reason for it. He always had a lesson about this unforgiving country.

'Don't come yet. It's too wet. You won't get far. This country has no bottom in it,' were George's first words of warning.

'George we've bought an old army Blitz. We should be right. It's got a 20 000-pound winch on it.'

'It's bloody wet, mate. We've had nine inches of rain. What else have you got?'

'An old Falcon ute and two bikes. That's all.'

'They might be all right if you don't go through the crust. Leave the Blitz at home.'

But we didn't. It was too late to pull the pin on the 550-kilometre trip from Brisbane at the last minute. Ray and I had booked the barge to co-ordinate with the tide – a couple of mates had arranged time off from work to help. I had attended to, and left, my business in safe hands. So we proceeded.

The *Robert Poulsen* delivered us to China Bay under difficult wet conditions, nearly beaching itself in the process. After disgorging its load, only under full throttle and seesawing backwards while sending up a mud boil did it slowly clear the mud shelf and drag itself back into deeper water. If it hadn't succeeded, it would've had a twelve-hour wait for the next high.

Stores unloaded, we were on our own. The Blitz drove fifty metres and then became bogged to the axles. It stayed bogged for three days. At times we managed to creep it along a few metres with the winch rope wrapped around a tree, or drive it a few centimetres under its own steam. And it rained heavily the whole time – something like nineteen inches. The 20 000-pound winch wasn't worth a cracker. All it did was lure us further into already impossible conditions – false security *that* turned out to be. Any advice that George gave about the weather, and anything else for that matter, was now followed to the letter.

Curtis Island is, in most cattlemen's evaluation, hard country. Sterile grey soil (useful for little more than holding up fence posts), rocks, sand and gnarled blackboys, genus *Xanthorrhea*, together make up about eighty per cent of the area. The landscape is relieved only here and there by stunted blue gum and innumerable species of hardy, windblown, coastal desperates that exist on salt spray and little else.

'Come up and I'll give you a look around Monte some time,' George offered soon after we'd settled in. So we did.

On the morning of our inspection of the western part of Monte, we were less than impressed.

'I don't know, George. Acre for acre, Monte Cristo is no better than our block, is it? It's only bigger,' I observed.

'Mostly not, mate,' he replied, but said nothing more.

It was rough and uncomfortable with the battered four-wheel-drive ute bouncing over interminable bush tracks, but it was worth it. Here and there, in pockets of better country, mobs of quality cattle stopped grazing and looked questioningly at our approach.

'Good cattle, George.'

'Yeah, most of them are. Taken a bit of getting them that way. I cull a lot.'

I detected pride in George's reserved manner. The only solitary cattle that we saw were lean, exhausted-looking bulls.

'Bugger of a life, eh? Root yourself stupid then go and have a sleep in the shade,' Kevin observed.

'Yeah, nice way of putting it,' George answered, smiling.

Random sightings of island wildlife caught our attention. Little companies of grey kangaroos bounded away in alarm, big families of black razorback pigs exploded from the dams in all directions, sorting themselves out on the run and snaking away in single files, brumby stallions with long manes snorted a challenge in surprised reflex then turned and herded their harems to safety, hurrying them along a bit with regular bruising bites on the rump; scrub cattle fairly bolted into the cover offering us barely a glimpse of their retreating forms; and a couple of dingoes assessed the situation and disappeared quick as a flash. The other wildlife was airborne: the odd wedge-tail with harrying crows in attendance; and thirty-two-and-a-half million sandflies; and only slightly fewer mozzies. A helicopter flying tourists to the converted Cape Capricorn Lighthouse away on the eastern seaboard completed the picture.

But we hadn't seen any really good country yet, and couldn't account for the good condition of the cattle.

'We'll go back and have lunch, then head out the other way. See what you think of that,' George offered.

An hour later we reboarded the rusty Cruiser and set off eastward for another bone-cracking ride on a rough track. And then we rounded a rocky knob and drove right onto a little brumby family and frightened the life out of them. The stallion showed strong traces of thoroughbred, although he was a lot smaller. He reminded me of the horse in Banjo's Paterson's classic line *'a touch of Timor pony – three parts thoroughbred at least . . .'.* Two very ordinary mares comprised his harem. One had a new foal at foot, and the other was apparently still suckling last year's colt, going by his beautiful condition and glossy coat.

'George, did one of your station sires get to a brumby mare a few years ago? That little stallion isn't a bad type.'

'No, mate. A lot of them aren't too bad.'

'Ever break one in?' I asked.

'Yeah, he was all right too.'

'Why don't you do it more often?'

'Too hit-and-miss, mate. Our way you get a good result all the time, or most times. Can't guarantee that with them.'

'Where's the good blood come from then?'

'This place was a remount breeding station for the British in India. Whenever the Brits got out of there – Christ knows when that was – there was no market for the remounts so they just opened the gate and turned them out, bushed them. Must be fifty years ago.'

'Yeah?'

'I've cleaned a lot up on Monte. You've still got a couple of hundred down your way.'

'Don't we know it. Have you ever run them?'

'Bugger a good horse chasing a crook one? Mug's game that one.'

'What about the chopper?'

'Yeah, been there done that. No good either. You can't bend them off their tracks. We even went right down and bumped them with the skids. Nearly knocked the chopper out of the air, if eight foot up is in the air.'

'*Shit, George! Look out!*'

'Hang on, we drop down steeply here. Hang on.'

Bumping, sliding, rearing up, dropping down . . . finally the country flattened and the nose of the Cruiser poked through the scrub.

'Holy bloody hell. Get a load of this!' I couldn't believe my eyes.

'Something, isn't it?' George said, nodding and smiling a little.

'Who'd have thought that this was in here?'

'Thought you'd be impressed.'

Stretching away as far as the eye could see to the north, east and south was a plain of magnificent country. Impressed? Hardly the word.

'How big is this, George?'

'Eleven thousand acres.'

'I thought I'd seen everything. Now I have.'

'Marine plain, mate. Run a lot of cattle out here. It holds the moisture. This good brown soil always does.'

There were cattle everywhere. God knows how many.

Big kindergartens of calves slept like babies in the shade of the trees surrounding the waterholes. They were all under the watchful eyes of a couple of nonchalant-looking aunties and their mothers, who rotated in order. To the untrained eye none of this would be apparent. One cow appeared in the distance coming towards the waterhole, another disappeared into the distance heading away from the waterhole. One had been relieved of her watch, another had come on duty.

Friendship groups of cows grazed along together – breeding-age heifers took the eyes of the bulls – part-grown steers surely ready to be transferred to the bullock paddock. I noted the look of satisfaction on George's face as he surveyed the scene before us. Cattleman, island cattleman, through and through, I thought.

Remembering all these moments I was suddenly anxious that George might not be able to continue doing what he loved. The accident should never have happened. The circumstances played over and over in my mind. Travelling alone I had plenty of uninterrupted time to think about it.

Completely out of the blue, with no warning whatsoever, our lease was curtailed after the first three-year period. Shattered wasn't a strong enough word. Not even a prior phone call – nothing, just a letter from a solicitor saying in effect, 'Vacate by 30 January. The property is to be sold.'

That gave us three months to finalise our occupation. And we were only just getting properly started . . .

I rang George. 'Mate, we've got the arse from our lease,' – and so on. After a bit of a talk – though not much because George isn't big on phones – we agreed on a course of action.

'I'll come and help you move out. You make the arrangements and let me know,' George offered.

At what might have been a 'fire sale' the property had sold quickly.

It was a big job organising to clear out, but before we got too far advanced, as good fortune would have it, the incoming freehold purchaser bought everything except the cattle and our saddles – all our gear, right down to the last nut and bolt. That helped no end.

'George, what do you think of a helicopter muster? Might make it easier.'

'Yeah, we don't use the chopper much except for scrubbers, but for your cattle and your country it will probably suit. They haven't been choppered before so they'll go pretty good. Some that have been continually mustered like that run into the scrub when they hear a chopper and stand stock-still, the cunning bastards. Set the date and I'll bring the horses down and bring a good ringer with me too.'

'Do you know anybody to fly for us?'

'Yeah, we have used Jimmy Crowson a bit. He's as good as any, might be better.'

'Good. That's what we'll do then. Have you got his number?'

He found it quickly and read it out. 'Okay, mate, just let me know. I'll come down when you're ready.' Then he rang off – you could say abruptly if you didn't know George.

Later we found out that it was standard practice for neighbours to attend a boundary muster anyway – to identify and claim any cattle that might have strayed either way.

The arrangements had all been made with the helicopter contractor, and then a few days before we were to start the muster the phone rang unusually early. It was Jimmy Crowson on the line and he was obviously upset. He'd rung to say his sister had just been killed mustering in one of his choppers out Clermont way and that he couldn't fly for us, that he'd never fly again. He finished by saying that he wouldn't leave us in the lurch and that he'd send a good lad, Kent Hansen, who would muster for us, but who had to do another job first.

Christ almighty, we were speechless – what news. Our hearts went out to people we didn't know. Was this a bad omen?

Kent Hansen, who looked like he was fifteen (he was actually twenty-two) came and mustered for us. What a daredevil! He'd fly in under the tree canopy, darting every which way, blowing dust all over the cattle and scaring the bejesus out of them, then come out half sideways as if he wasn't even looking. I'd never witnessed anything like it.

The first day's flying was most productive, and we yarded probably three-quarters of the herd. But it hadn't been without drama. A recalcitrant beast had broken from the mob and made a desperate bid for freedom across the mudflats – innocuous looking terrain to the uninitiated, but treacherous and respected by the experienced.

At the time, George was tailing the small mob in the shadow of the chopper. Astride his smart little mare he gave chase, attempting to campdraft the breakaway before the animal gained the water. It probably planned to swim to a neighbouring island, as some were wont to do at low tide, in quest of the sweet and nutritious herbage that grew there in season. But this wasn't low tide and the animal took a risk to attempt it.

So George rode onto the young scrubber bull, grabbed it by the tail and spurred his horse forward to pull it off balance and over. Normally he would have had a strap around his waist to tie up the beast, but today he hadn't predicted the need.

Meanwhile, Kent had witnessed the catch, but not immediately the sequel. As the chopper banked, Kent could see George was in trouble. He'd sprung off, immobilised the steer and went to tie it with the surcingle off his saddle (which he had deftly unbuckled and slid out while still holding the animal). That should have worked, but it didn't. The strap slipped off its muddy hoof so George loosened the horse's girth strap and slid the saddle blanket out from under the saddle. And that's all he had to capture the beast with as it rose to its feet. There he was, in the middle of nowhere, holding the bull's horns through the blanket and looking plaintively into the air for assistance. There was a real risk of the beast attacking him if it could see him. You could say that he had the bull by the horns – twice.

Incredibly, the spotter, sitting next to Kent in the tiny Robinson, had witnessed none of the drama on the ground, as he had been concentrating on what he was supposed to be doing. So when Kent dropped the chopper out of the sky like a stone, sprang out and took off, the spotter (who still hadn't noticed George and his dilemma) thought he'd better do the same, fearing some impending disaster. A fixed-wing pilot himself, he knew all about avgas. So he ripped off his seatbelt, bailed out the other side and tore off in the opposite direction towards the thin scrub. He was rather sheepish when he turned, looked back and saw Kent grab the beast by the tail and throw it the second time.

What a day!

That evening in the camp, for the want of something better to say to the young pilot, who'd palled up with my eighteen-year-old son, Dan, I asked, 'Where was your last job, mate? Jimmy said there was one in front of us.'

He drew a breath and didn't say a word for a moment. I wondered, *surely he can answer, what's his go?*

Finally he gulped and said, 'It was the hardest thing I've ever done in my life. I had to fly over Jimmy's sister's funeral and empty out buckets of rose petals at the graveside.'

'Geez, sorry, mate.' I felt a pang of guilt having thought that his hesitation a few moments ago was due to his being less than well mannered.

He simply nodded, accepting the apology, but I could tell by his demeanour that it hadn't been necessary.

George's wife, the irrepressible little Joy, and Ray's wife, the happy-go-lucky Robyn, had excelled themselves and roasted a couple of big joints of beef to feed the mob, ten of us in all. There wasn't a scrap left, bearing testimony to their skills.

After accepting compliments about their culinary prowess,

Robyn was eager to make a point. 'You fellows think you're the only ones who can cook in an outside galley. I reckon we do a better job than all of you.'

'Steady on there, Rob. Don't be too rash,' Ray advised with a cheerful smirk.

'You lot all stand around drinking stubbies while the bum gets burnt out of everything.'

'Sheesh, what have we done to deserve this?'

'Only joking.'

I thought a change of subject might be in order. 'Have you ever run many scrubbers, George?'

'Yeah, and mostly down here before you blokes shifted in. They're Monte cattle gone wild. Some of them still wear a Monte brand.'

'We've seen plenty, but only cleanskins so far. Tell you what I have seen, and that's a saddle horse running with the brumbies. He has a saddle mark on his wither.'

'Yeah, mate. There was a clown at Southend a few years ago going to start a riding school. A couple of his horses died and he bushed that one. The brumbies let him in because he was a gelding. If he'd been a stallion they would have killed him.'

'What about the scrub bulls, George? Ever had any close calls?'

'No, not really. They're no match for a pack of enthusiastic dogs, and I've got plenty of them.'

He was right about that because I'd counted twenty-seven – even though there was a litter of five newborns in the tally.

'Got to have plenty. Their life expectancy is a bit less than those little lap-dogs you see sitting in front of the telly eating dog chocolates,' he said and smiled.

'What about scrub cows? Will they box up with quiet cattle?'

'No, I don't want them near the breeders. Spoil the mob – they're probably carrying the diseases we're trying to control. No, we barge them straight off to the works.'

'They'd probably be a bit easier to handle than the bulls, wouldn't they?'

'No way, mate. I'd sooner step off to a bull any day. They're predictable – cows aren't.'

'Why aren't I surprised?' I offered.

'Don't let the women hear that or you'll be the cook in the morning.'

Daylight was heralded noisily by the whoof-whoof-whoof of the chopper blades. Kent had fuelled up and kicked the engine into life to warm it up. Without any aviation experience whatsoever I thought there might be some technical rigmarole to observe or checklists to adhere to or flight plan to lodge, but he made it seem just so ordinary – hand pump a bit of fuel into the tank and turn the key. That was all I saw, but of course he could have been up earlier.

George and his ringer, Lennie, were already mounted, Ray was strapped into the spotter's seat and my crew were all aboard the Blitz to make the 20-kilometre road trip across the island to where our horses had been left yarded the night before.

The chopper would put together the mob and add to it all along the way. Lennie and George would work on the ground for the fifteen or so cross-country kilometres to the western side of the island. We'd pick up the mob as they neared the yards and be ready for the scrub dash to secure any cleanskins that had never been anywhere near stockyards and might be boxed up with the mob. Hopefully they'd all be fairly weary by then. The horses loved this wild stuff and so did we.

As we arrived one horse snickered a low greeting and another followed suit. But I think it may have been the bag of workhorse mix they were welcoming. We would have a long wait before we saw any action, so we fed them their breakfast, took them down to water and hobbled them out for a few hours to let them feed around. When they stopped foraging and started to droop in the shade we threw the saddles on and waited – and waited. It was after smoko before we picked up the first intermittent chopper sounds. They were still a long way off even then. Finally we rode out, two of us each side of the track that led into the wings and funnelled into the yards, but well back off it so as not to spook the cattle. As it came closer the chopper's constant change in pitch suggested it was really working hard. Maybe the cattle were still troublesome, although they'd hardly have much sting left in them after the long, fast walk across the island. Or maybe Kent had a bigger mob than I'd anticipated. We'd soon see. But then a thought crossed my mind. Perhaps Kent was having difficulty drafting off the little mobs of brumbies that had probably raced away in front of the cattle all the way. They'd never been anywhere near the yards either and would have been starting to realise that they were well off their territory. Lennie confirmed that later.

But for the moment the leaders, still a good way off, were gradually materialising through the scrub. As they became more distinct, we couldn't see any brumbies, just the lead bullocks. The chopper darted back and forth above and behind them. Then, without warning and simple as you like, it dropped into the scrub. One second it was there – one eye blink and it wasn't.

'Fuckin' hell it's crashed! It's gone down. Come on, you blokes.'

Unbeknown to us, the pilot had reacted to a drama unfolding on the ground. George's beautiful little mare, at an easy canter, had tripped in a concealed hole. She stumbled forward and tried to regain her footing. Twice George nearly bailed out, but in the last split-second, made the decision to stay with her. It was a bad choice. She went down headfirst, somersaulting right over and landing on top of George. Ray said later it all seemed to take place in slow motion. Lennie was there first and sprang off his horse while it was still at the canter. He couldn't shift George's horse by himself. She was out cold although at that moment Lennie thought she was dead – and that George wasn't long for this world either.

Ray and the pilot sprang from the cockpit as soon as they'd touched down. They sprinted neck and neck to help Lennie pull the horse off George. But I hadn't been able to see what was going on and I was convinced that the chopper had crashed and would be a burning wreckage at any moment. It didn't register that the rotor blades were still spinning at what was probably a normal idle. Relief flooded through me when I saw Ray and the pilot emerge from the bush about sixty metres away but I became quickly mystified as they dashed back into it a little further along. At least I now knew that nobody in the chopper had been hurt, however, the urgency of their movements panicked me and I spurred Cheeky into a flat sprint. On approaching, I could see the horse on the ground, but couldn't see George. I shot out of the saddle and hit the ground running. A second later my blood ran cold when I spotted his legs sticking out from under his beloved little mare. Just then she started to regain consciousness and Ray bellowed, 'Come on, all together. *Heave!*' and she was off George.

'Keep going. Don't let her fall back on him. Steady now girl, easy now. Christ! Push her over the other way. Push her arse over head if you have to!'

'George, how bad are you?' Lennie was down on his knees beside him.

'Don't move me: I'm broken below the waist. Get some help,' he whispered weakly between clenched teeth.

The cattle had scattered, any scrubbers gone west – or north or south or somewhere else – and there was no sign of a brumby. Kent was looking at me, frowning, and mouthing a request for instructions.

'Fly back over to Gladstone and ask the agent to get onto Lloyds to bring their big Medivac chopper – fast. Tell them to send a doctor, he's been crushed by a horse. How long will it take you to fly across the harbour?'

'About five minutes.'

'Good. Radio through and tell them you're coming.'

Kent was in the air within fifteen seconds and then we just had to wait. It was stinking hot – the hottest part of the day in the hottest month of the year. George was sweating profusely and we tried to keep the sun off him with a saddle blanket. He wanted water, but Lennie just dribbled a bit into his mouth, saying he'd done first aid and George shouldn't have much. He lay there ashen-faced, in shock, and bit on his doubled-over left forefinger, not making a sound. His bladder had let go and I don't think he was even aware of it. I didn't like the look of this at all.

About half an hour had passed and nobody had turned up. George would die here, at our feet, if he didn't get help soon. Concern coupled with a feeling of helplessness welled up in us. We had to keep George awake. Lennie kept talking continuously and making George answer.

'George, George, stay awake, mate.'

'Lennie keep going, keep talking,' I urged.

'George, don't go to sleep mate. We've got to cross those weaners remember.' George was lapsing in and out of consciousness.

'We've got to muster the plain, George. Stay with us mate, stay with us.'

But George was becoming less responsive. We were losing him.

Ray turned to me, 'Rhylle, take the four-wheel drive to Southend and phone to see what's wrong at the hospital. Pick up Robyn and Joy on your way back. No, better than that, ask Joy to bring her little Suzuki. We might need it. Get them to come back here before you go in to ring up.'

'Yeah,' Lennie said. 'Better for Joy to be here as soon as possible.'

His look was alarming.

Finally there was something I could do that might help. I drove the twenty-odd kilometres at breakneck speed across the island to the camp. No professional rally driver could have covered the country quicker. Alerting the women to what had happened I continued the four kilometres on to Southend to get to the phone.

I rang the hospital and fell out with them. They told me they couldn't despatch the big chopper because they couldn't find any George Wilson as a paid-up member of the air ambulance. I shared a few thoughts of mine concerning their ancestry and finished up by saying that we'd foot the bill if he wasn't paid up.

'Okay, sir. Now that's cleared up we'll send the helicopter right away.'

'And send a doctor too. This bloke is hurt pretty bad.'

'We'll see what we can do, sir.' Click.

Bastards! Here's a working man not too far off dying, who actually contributes to the community and they won't send a chopper till they find out whether he's paid up or not. Geez the bastards give me the shits. I was cursing out loud, but cooled down slightly as I drove back and once again focused on what we could do to help. By the time I'd returned, the big chopper had just landed in a huge clearing nowhere near George. Kent had come back with them to identify the accident site. He was absolutely appalled that the pilot wouldn't land right beside George. In his opinion the Medivac pilot shouldn't have had a licence if he couldn't land in the little clearing close by. Of course, this *was* the opinion of a daredevil young mustering pilot . . . I was relieved to see the medivac chopper on the ground and at that moment didn't give the ambulance subscription mix-up another thought. More pressing problems had to be addressed.

I was horrified that they hadn't sent a doctor. They'd sent an ambulance officer who, after giving George the summary once-over, decided that he was only severely bruised. The ambo wasn't able to administer any pain-killers, so after his diagnosis he simply oversaw our handling of George and helped us lift him up onto the tray of the Cruiser, then we bumped him out cross-country to the big chopper some distance away. My heart went out to George. He was absolutely white, and so was Joy, and although he must have been in agony, he didn't make a sound. There had been some relief with the diagnosis, but bruising seemed such a minor result for such a major fall. We rolled him onto a stretcher and loaded him into the Medivac chopper with Joy and then they were gone. A hollow feeling overtook me as we watched the chopper until it was just a speck in the sky. Then, subdued and saddened, we attended to the cattle we'd mustered the day before. This was a terrible end to such an exciting muster. Upon discussion, we all very much doubted the diagnosis, especially Lennie, who'd seen the accident happen. He was adamant that there would have to be some internal injury.

After he arrived at the hospital George was left out on the verandah, unattended, for a couple of hours. Maybe he had to wait for the right doctor – who knows. He told me later he thought they'd forgotten about him. When I queried their laxity he replied, 'Doesn't matter, mate. They're treating me pretty good now. I'll be as fat as a pig when I get out of here. Don't worry about it, mate.'

His injuries included two broken hips and a broken pelvis, among other less serious fractures and bruises. The doctor told George that if the break in the pelvis had been dead centre his body would have split like a melon and he'd have died within a few minutes. He was absolutely aghast at the treatment George had suffered getting to hospital. It could very easily have killed him. He shouldn't have been moved before professional assessment. Of course, that was easy to say after the event.

A month later Ray and Lennie mustered and crossed George's weaners over to the mainland. He was most grateful.

And George himself? Well he was in hospital for months, then home and on light duties for nearly a year. Amazingly, he regularly sat on an empty 200-litre drum suspended lengthways between the tank stand and the clothes hoist to regain his saddle posture. He invested in a custom-made saddle and graduated to horseback, then short musters, longer ones and finally full days. That all took two years.

Today he's still the boss of Monte Cristo, still the quiet, unassuming working man who loves what he does and does it well. Money is not his motivation – good cattle, good horses, good dogs are, as is the magnificent presentation of Monte's annual turn-off.

ROB HUGHES

Stranger on the shore

—•◦•—

I'd lost track of the date, though I knew that it was sometime in August. This was nothing new – I've been buggering around most of my life. Once again I was out chasing rainbows and min-min lights, crossing dry gullies, this time, trying to write a book. My wife, Karyn, and I were in our trusty little Hilux ute, taking some of the roads less travelled on the way westward to Alice Springs and Uluru in the Northern Territory via the northern outskirts of the Simpson Desert. Our daughter, Kylie, and her fiancé, Mick, were following in their twin-cab, along with our youngest son, Dan.

Our first destination was the newest and most remote national park in Queensland, Diamantina Lakes, situated in the Channel country of south-west Queensland's semiarid area. All of us being very much at home in the bush we chose to camp rough – close to nature and for safety reasons far off the beaten track.

Night travel was never an option. The risk of a collision with a kangaroo was too great. Having a broken-legged, two-metre kangaroo up over the bonnet, through the windscreen and into the cab didn't appeal to many drivers. There's only one thing worse than having a dead kangaroo in the cab, and that's having a half-dead one. We knew it happened often enough.

Our beds were swags out under the stars, and our five-star restaurant meals were from the camp oven. No TV. On the first day we had a good camp set up outside Mitchell well before sundown.

Intermittent radio reports kept us in touch with the latest news, and let us know how the world was getting on without us.

The latest bulletin was disturbing. A battered girl had waved down a couple of road-train drivers on a lonely section of highway and told them an alarming story. The Kombi van driven by her boyfriend had been pulled over by a lone male on the pretext that there was something wrong with the back of it. She'd alleged that she'd heard a gunshot from behind the Kombi, and then her boyfriend had disappeared. She had then been trussed up with a variety of bondage from which she'd escaped. The truckies found her to be seriously traumatised. The person responsible was still at large.

'We'll have to be careful with our camps, but I suppose we've got safety in numbers,' Mick offered.

'I don't usually say this too loudly, but I've got my little under-and-over rifle under the seat,' I admitted.

'You didn't bring that, surely?' Karyn asked.

'Always.'

'You've never said anything before,' she looked at me, almost accusingly.

'Never had to. Just thought I'd say something now to make you feel a little more secure at night.'

'What if the police found out?'

'They'd probably think I was the abductor. If that girl's story

147

is true and there's some deranged maniac on the loose, you'll be thanking me before this trip's over.'

Next day saw us continuing west through Quilpie and into the rich Channel country where, seasonally, the rivers run inland. The waters are bound for Lake Eyre, but rarely reach their destination.

That night the camp-fire talk waxed and waned.

In the background, some bloke was singing about two or three blokes coming to town and getting on the booze.

'Jesus, I'm getting sick of that bloody tune, Dan. Haven't you got anything else?'

'I like it.'

'So did I the first fifty times.'

He took the hint and turned off the tape player. Silence settled over us as we sat gazing into the camp fire, lost in our own thoughts.

The following morning we tidied up in no time.

'Hurry up. Let's get this show on the road,' I urged.

'Don't be so impatient, Dad. We're on holidays you know,' Dan answered as he scrabbled through a shoebox full of loose cassettes.

Our route took us through a couple of big stations. Their roads were good enough by western Queensland standards, maintained by a single grader pass every twelve months or so, whether they needed it or not.

Around midday a dust plume rose up on the horizon in front of us. It provided a focus on otherwise monotonous downs country. Good cattle country.

'Probably a road train . . . have to be by the dust storm he's putting up,' I remarked. 'He's closing fast and we've got no speed up. He must be giving it a boot full.'

And so he was – so they were, more likely.

'Rhylle pull over quickly. Let them go,' Karyn yelled at me.

'Jesus Christ, they're flying.'

It was no road train. It was a police car closely followed by a paddy wagon. 'Go you bastards. Hope you run into a radar trap,' I shouted out the window as dust engulfed us.

'Wind the window up,' Karyn said. 'You're full of bulldust and now the cab is too.'

By midafternoon we'd reached Diamantina Lakes. As we made camp, the dry weather meant puffs of dust at every footstep. Spindly gidgee trees filtered the relentless sun, creating sparse shade patches. These became momentarily coveted and the playful competition for them brought us out in a sweat. The esky became more popular than ever.

In no time at all practised routines had the camp shipshape and we all relaxed in the shade. Dan and Mick had a swim, and were clean until they clambered up the bank through knee-deep mud that surrounded the low coffee-coloured water.

Eyeing the drying mud Kylie said, 'That's quite a fashion statement Mick. The girls from St Rita's wear brown stockings, but they usually wear them with lace-ups not double pluggers.'

'Better not forget to take them off before I get into the old fart-sack tonight,' said Mick, making himself comfortable on a banana lounge.

The shrinking waterholes teemed with tiny fish and concentrated bird life took advantage of the harvest. Pelicans formed circles and drove the shoals to shallow water, feasting on them till they were stuffed. Forlorn-looking cormorants perched on rocks waiting for their wings to dry out – they'd also had their fill. And tall skinny waders stalked the shallows and secured their meal by spearing, using their long necks as woomeras.

Later as the camp came to life after the afternoon siesta, the sun, affected by smoke from a distant fire, seemed to set early into a crimson ball and created an unexpected panorama.

It was another fairly quiet camp that night.

By smoko next morning there was washing flapping in the breeze, a billy boiling, the tantalising smell of damper, and Lee Kernaghan was belting out 'Boys from the Bush'. Then, between track changes, I picked up the distant sound of a vehicle approaching and turned to focus on a dust trail. As it drew closer we could see that it was a station wagon. The first thing that sprang to mind was that the gunman on the loose had reportedly departed the scene of his crime in a wagon.

'I wonder who we've got here,' I said to anyone close enough to hear.

Paranoid? Perhaps. Cautious? Certainly. A hundred metres off, the wagon slowed yet kept rolling towards us. I stood beside the open door of the Hilux and watched the vehicle approach, taking note of where each of our party was.

It was a Landrover Discovery, but that didn't really mean anything.

Slowly, it turned in at 90 degrees and came to a halt about forty metres away.

It was a long moment before the driver alighted, and an even longer one as he stood without further movement. It was hard to see anything more from that distance. Eventually, the driver emerged from behind the Landrover and halted briefly at the rear of the vehicle as if he might open the tailgate. He appeared to be alone and was unhurried but purposeful in his movements. He simply brushed his hand over the paintwork at the back as if feeling for a dent or scratch and walked towards us.

He had nothing in his hand. Thank Christ for that. Still, I was a little wary. The others had ceased their various camp activities and were trying to look nonchalant as they quietly observed the newcomer's approach – trying not to be seen as a line of Brown's cows looking over the fence.

'G'day, mate,' Mick said. 'Come far?'

'Only a hundred kilometres this morning. I put my daughter on a plane in Mt Isa the other day. Been on my own since. You all seem settled in. Nice spot. Better if there was a bit more water.'

I pushed the door closed. We'd all relaxed somewhat after he spoke.

'Anyway, I'm Rob Hughes,' he said extending a hand.

Friendly, I thought. I noted his hands weren't calloused and rough like my own.

'I'm Rhylle.'

'I'm Karyn.'

'I'm Kylie – and these two tall skinny . . . er . . . fellas are Mick and Dan.'

'G'day, mate.'

'How'yer goin'?'

'We're just having a cup of tea and a slab of damper. Any good to you?' I asked.

'Yes, that would be nice. That damper looks good and smells even better. Thank you.'

'Why did you pull up over there mate?' Mick asked.

'Well, I thought that if I came roaring in billowing dust you might not offer me a cup of tea.'

He spoke in a quiet, cultured voice that seemed out of place in the bush, and in comparison I thought my own speech was somewhat rough and ready.

I said, 'How considerate. Not many would even think of doing that. You'd be right about the lack of an invite if our damper was dusted with dirt instead of flour. Might have told you to . . . er . . . depart these environs without further ado.'

He laughed, a casual easy laugh, 'No, I'm careful not to offend anyone. It's pretty lonely out here. And it wouldn't do to put anyone offside. Never know when you might need a hand.'

I was warming to him quickly. I even felt a bit sheepish about thinking that he may have posed some threat.

Kylie handed him a steaming mug of tea and a thick slice of warm, crusty damper liberally laced with golden syrup and he continued, 'I was hoping that you mightn't mind if I camp nearby. I had a bad experience last night and it's unsettled me. I was camped well off the road and thought I was safe. Would have been too, only some pig shooters came through close by.'

'Few bullets whistling around?'

'Yes, and they had spotlights too, but they didn't notice my little green tent because it must have blended in with the bush.'

'Lucky you didn't have a couple of pigs hiding in there with you,' Dan said.

'I very nearly did. They were crackling about on the dry twigs all around me . . . poor choice of words there I feel,' he added with a wry grin.

Mick chuckled, 'Could have had plenty of crackling if you'd still had your fire going. You're big enough to wrestle a good size pig for the spit.'

Rob looked a little taken aback.

'Sorry mate,' Mick back-pedalled. 'It probably scared the arse off you. It would've me.'

'It did. For a start, with the spotlights through the trees, I thought it was the min-min. I hoped I might be lucky enough to get a sighting. They've never hurt anyone, have they?' asked Rob.

'Don't think so,' I answered. 'We saw one down near Birdsville once. Scared the bejesus out of us. We weren't pissed either. Couldn't get to sleep after it. None of us could. It wasn't that we were afraid, but it left us all with a peculiar feeling inside . . . like we'd been half-electrocuted.'

'Dunno about that one, Dad,' said Kylie. 'You're either electrocuted or you aren't. It's like saying someone's half pregnant.'

'Okay. Half . . . stunned then, or something.'

I turned to Rob. 'Yeah, mate. Camp anywhere you like. We're all pretty harmless. The only bush pigs around here are standing right beside you.'

'You'll keep,' Mick muttered, and Dan mouthed something that indicated a certain lack of respect towards his father.

'What a life,' Dan said, 'I think I'll get a stubby. Want one, Mick?'

'Is the Pope a Catholic?'

We spent the afternoon lazing about, dozing then cooling off – in the lake or the esky – reading in the shade near the water's edge, yarning to our new friend or watching pelicans fishing. Rob seemed a nice bloke. He'd been a primary school principal down in Sydney or somewhere, and had retired.

He told us, 'Ali, my daughter, and I did a trip across the Simpson Desert with a few friends a couple of weeks ago, but she had to go back to uni, so I decided to go on alone. I'm not sure, yet, that it was the right decision.'

'Ah, you'll be right, mate.'

We'd all been a bit careful about what we said until we'd learned that he was a schoolteacher, but then he and Karyn were in deep discussion about the comparative education systems of New South Wales and Queensland. Teachers can't help talking shop whenever they meet. I am an authority on the subject. My brother is a teacher, my two sisters are, my sister-in-law is, and so is my wife. I'm sur-rounded by them, they're every bloody where. No wonder a bloke takes off into the desert, but even there he's not safe.

As the afternoon progressed, Rob was turning out to be a well-read, well-travelled, interesting bloke with a great command of the English language. Some of his gentler stories contrasted with some of my more robust ones – overall a good balance, I thought. I was beginning to feel that we were lucky he happened along.

I tried to do a little writing, but it degenerated into nonsense because I didn't have my heart in it. A few lines of rhyming doggerel were the result of half an afternoon. Holiday mode had taken over.

At about four o'clock Mick started busying about chopping wood and rattling pots and pans.

'You the cook tonight?' I asked. 'You know if you keep doing such a good job we won't let you stop.'

'I think I'll be able to stop whenever I like. I always keep a packet of Epsom salts in my first aid kit for emergencies just like that.'

'All right, all right, point taken. I'll cook when it's my turn, although I have a poem by Tom Quilty you might like to hear first.'

I leant on the post-hole shovel that we used to stoke the coals in the fire, and recited the poem.

The drover's cook weighed fifteen stone,
He had one bloodshot eye,
He had no laces in his boots,
No buttons on his fly.

His pants hung loosely round his hips,
Hitched by a piece of wire,
They concertina'd round his boots,
In a way that you'd admire.

He stuck the billy on to boil,
Then emptied out his pipe,
And with his greasy shirt sleeve,
He gave his nose a wipe.

With pipe in mouth he mixed a sod,
A drip hung from his chin,

And as he mixed the damper up,
The drip kept dripping in.

'A cook,' I said, 'you call yourself,
You dirty slop-made lout.
You should be jailed for taking work
You cannot carry out.'

Rob was impressed, so he said. However his demeanour didn't quite seem to match his words.

'Do you write a bit of poetry? Is that one of yours?' he asked.

'No, mate. I do write for a living, but that one isn't mine.'

'No, his is a lot worse than that, if it's possible,' Kylie interrupted.

'Actually, the publishers told me that I should stop trying to write poetry, that it's shit and pulls the rest of my writing down. I thought it was helping to keep it up.'

Mick brought the conversation back to the present. 'I think I'd rather keep on doing the cooking, Rhylle. You remind me too much of that bloke in your poem.'

'Banned from cooking,' I said, pretending to look hurt, then added, 'I'm not as stupid as I look, you know.'

'There's always the washing up. You need the practice, according to your wife.'

A little later, at sundown, we gathered around the fire and made ourselves comfortable. I opened a bottle of good red wine for Karyn and Kylie. Mick prodded the meat and Dan went to turn the vegies in the camp ovens – springing back as he got spattered. Rob Hughes came over from his vehicle with a tin of stew to heat for his tea.

Mick said, 'Bloody hell, put that back in your truck, mate. Didn't any of these buggers invite you for dinner?'

'I thought you did,' I said to Karyn.

'I thought you did,' Kylie said to Dan.

'Well let's make it official. Would you like to join us for our evening repast, Robert?' Mick said formally.

'Certainly, my friend. I should be delighted. At what hour might it be convenient for me to arrive?'

'How about now, since you're already here. Drag up a stump.'

Rob opened the conversation, 'I've just been speaking to my wife on the satellite phone.'

'You've got your vehicle really well equipped,' Mick said as he handed Rob a stubby. 'I'd like a setup like that one day. We're out of range on the mobile here.'

Rob nodded his thanks and went on, 'Julia has just been giving me an update about the abduction of that English tourist. Have you heard it's now a murder investigation?'

Everyone turned to listen.

'There's still no sign of the boyfriend, Peter Falconio, and the police have blocked the media from making any contact with the girl. Makes you feel rather vulnerable with a suspected murderer out there somewhere.'

'Yeah, mate, you're not wrong,' I agreed. 'I hate to tell you this, but we looked pretty hard at you when you first turned up.'

'No offence taken,' he answered. 'It pays to be careful. I must admit I would have kept driving if you weren't obviously a family.'

Dan piped up, 'How much longer will that roast be, Mick?'

'Rhylle, I can't stop thinking about that dirty cook. You've put me off my dinner,' Karyn said, then added, 'but that poem just suits you. Your style . . . er . . . the way you think . . . Oh, you know what I mean.'

'Actually I have no idea. That's nice, isn't it? Turning on your lifelong partner and soul mate over a bit of verse, albeit verse lacking a little in quality. I question your integrity. *Avez vous* been living a lie, *ma chérie*?'

'Have you been drinking?'

'*Non madame*, not at all. You are well acquainted with my temperate habits.'

Dan turned on me too. 'Shit, Dad, you're carrying on as if you've only got one oar in the water.'

'*Excusé moi*, one and all, but I must depart for *une oui oui*.'

A little later a magnificent baked dinner stopped the rot and quietened the camp for an hour.

I looked at my watch and was surprised to find that it was only 8.30 p.m. I thought it would have been later.

'Come on you lot,' I urged, 'let's crank this party up a bit. Anyone got a banjo in their swag?'

Kylie said, 'Speaking of banjos, I really like *The Man from Snowy River* – the original one. It's a great poem. Truly Australian.'

Dan said, 'It's my favourite too. Have to be I suppose. It's the only one I know.'

'I agree. Would you like to hear it?' Rob volunteered and looked about expectantly.

I've heard some pretty poor attempts at *The Man* – even from accomplished bush poets. I quietly hoped he wouldn't murder it.

The kettle whistling in the background reassured me that if it got too painful I could call for a coffee break.

Karyn piped up, 'Please go ahead. I think it's everyone's favourite.' She wasn't missing an opportunity to hear his rendition.

I glanced across at Kylie who discreetly raised one eyebrow. I could see she shared my fears. In the half dark Dan sat on the end of a log with a glazed-eyed schoolboy look.

And Rob began . . .

There was movement at the station, for the word had passed around
That the colt from old Regret had got away,
And had joined the wild bush horses – he was worth a
thousand pound,
So all the cracks had gathered to the fray.
All the tried and noted riders from the stations near and far
Had mustered at the homestead overnight,
For the bushmen love hard riding where the wild bush horses are,
And the stock-horse snuffs the battle with delight.

There was Harrison, who made his pile when Pardon won the cup,
The old man with his hair as white as snow;
But few could ride beside him when his blood was fairly up –
He would go wherever horse and man could go.
And Clancy of the Overflow came down to lend a hand,
No better horseman ever held the reins;
For never horse could throw him while the saddle girths
would stand –
He learnt to ride while droving on the plains.

I'd never heard a rendition begin like this. The vibrancy and timbre of Rob's voice perfectly matched the rhythm of Banjo's creation. I shook my head and looked at Karyn. Her face said it all. We were enthralled.

And one was there, a stripling on a small and weedy beast;
He was something like a racehorse undersized,
With a touch of Timor pony – three parts thoroughbred
   at least –
And such as are by mountain horsemen prized.
He was hard and tough and wiry – just the sort that won't say die –
There was courage in his quick impatient tread;
And he bore the badge of gameness in his bright and fiery eye,
And the proud and lofty carriage of his head.

But still so slight and weedy, one would doubt his power to stay,
And the old man said, 'That horse will never do
For a long and tiring gallop – lad, you'd better stop away,
Those hills are far too rough for such as you.'
So he waited, sad and wistful – only Clancy stood his friend –
'I think we ought to let him come,' he said;
'I warrant he'll be with us when he's wanted at the end,
For both his horse and he are mountain bred.'

My mind had been transported. *Let him go, please let him go!* It was as if I didn't know the answer. It could have been me in the saddle. I wanted it to be me.

He hails from Snowy River, up by Kosciusko's side,
Where the hills are twice as steep and twice as rough;
Where a horse's hoofs strike firelight from the flint stones
 every stride,
The man that holds his own is good enough.
And the Snowy River riders on the mountains make their home,
Where the river runs those giant hills between;
I have seen full many horsemen since I first commenced to roam,
But nowhere yet such horsemen have I seen.'

So he went; they found the horses by the big mimosa clump,
They raced away towards the mountain's brow,
And the old man gave his orders, 'Boys, go at them from the jump,
No use to try for fancy riding now.
And, Clancy, you must wheel them, try and wheel them to
 the right.
Ride boldly, lad, and never fear the spills,
For never yet was rider that could keep the mob in sight,
If once they gain the shelter of those hills.'

So Clancy rode to wheel them – he was racing on the wing
Where the best and boldest riders take their place,
And he raced his stock-horse past them, and he made the
 ranges ring
With the stockwhip, as he met them face to face.
Then they halted for a moment, while he swung the
 dreaded lash,
But they saw their well-loved mountain full in view,

And they charged beneath the stockwhip with a sharp and
  sudden dash,
And off into the mountain scrub they flew.

Now I was there riding with them, my heart pounding in time with
the hoofbeats, and such was the pace that the wind whipped across
my face and tipped the brim of my hat upwards. I was possessed,
in another world – the high country.

Then fast the horsemen followed, where the gorges deep and black
Resounded to the thunder of their tread,
And the stockwhips woke the echoes, and they fiercely
  answered back
From cliffs and crags that beetled overhead.
And upward, ever upward, the wild horses held their way,
Where mountain ash and kurrajong grew wide;
And the old man muttered fiercely, 'We may bid the mob good day,
No man can hold them down the other side.'

When they reached the mountain's summit, even Clancy
  took a pull,
It well might make the boldest hold their breath;
The wild hop scrub grew thickly, and the hidden ground was full
Of wombat holes, and any slip was death.
But the man from Snowy River let the pony have his head,
And he swung his stockwhip round and gave a cheer,
And he raced him down the mountain like a torrent down its bed,
While the others stood and watched in very fear.

I was riding now for Clancy – riding hard and riding rough to make him proud – the small and weedy beast belting headlong through the scrub, all caution to the wind.

He sent the flint-stones flying, but the pony kept his feet,
He cleared the fallen timber in his stride,
And the man from Snowy River never shifted in his seat –
It was grand to see that mountain horseman ride.
Through the stringybarks and saplings, on the rough and
*   broken ground,*
Down the hillside at a racing pace he went;
And he never drew the bridle till he landed safe and sound,
At the bottom of that terrible descent.

He was right among the horses as they climbed the further hill,
And the watchers on the mountain, standing mute,
Saw him ply the stockwhip fiercely, he was right among them still,
As he raced across the clearing in pursuit.
Then they lost him for a moment, where two mountain gullies met
In the ranges, but a final glimpse reveals
On a dim and distant hillside the wild horses racing yet,
With the man from Snowy River at their heels.

And he ran them single-handed till their sides were white with foam.
He followed like a bloodhound on their track,
Till they halted, cowed and beaten, then he turned their heads
*   for home,*
And alone and unassisted brought them back.

But his hardy mountain pony he could scarcely raise a trot,
He was blood from hip to shoulder from the spur;
But his pluck was still undaunted, and his courage fiery hot,
For never yet was mountain horse a cur.

Exhausted, my heart still beat wildly. I felt as one with the man from Snowy River. I had never ridden so well. I didn't want this ride to end.

And down by Kosciusko, where the pine-clad ridges raise
Their torn and rugged battlements on high,
Where the air is clear as crystal, and the white stars fairly blaze
At midnight in the cold and frosty sky,
And where around The Overflow the reed-beds sweep and sway
To the breezes, and the rolling plains are wide,
The Man from Snowy River is a household word today,
And the stockmen tell the story of his ride.

As Rob finished, there was a moment of complete silence. Disbelief. Then the spell was broken. I felt so privileged. The audience might have numbered only five but the ovation surely indicated a hundred – a standing ovation, no less.

It might have been the setting; it might have been the camp fire; it might have been the mood and the timing, but it was probably all of that and more. There was no way the recitation could have been bettered. Rob delivered the poem with such passion, such energy and such rhythm that we were utterly captivated. It was an experience I'd never forget.

I extended my hand towards him and said, 'Rob Hughes, you are very welcome in our camp my friend. That was magnificent. I've never heard anything like that, and I've heard it recited a thousand times.'

'That must have taken years of practice, Rob,' Karyn said. 'I bet your students all loved you. I'm totally impressed. I think I need another drink.'

'Me too,' Kylie added.

'Yeah, Dan, I'll have one too while you're in the esky,' Mick said. 'We'll have to have a toast to that. You want one Banjo? Clancy? Whoever you are? Dan, get Clancy here one too.'

'To Rob Hughes,' the toast rang out.

'To the Man from Snowy River,' said Kylie.

'And his horse,' Dan added.

'Yeah, to his horse. To the small and weedy beast.'

We drank to them all.

'I can't believe I thought you might have been the desert murderer, Rob,' I said. 'Only joking mate.'

Rob smiled, 'And I thought you lot might have had something to do with it. Only joking mate.'

We laughed.

'It's a bloody worry, though, isn't it,' I added.

'Come on,' Mick said, 'let's get on with the concert. Who's next?'

'You,' Kylie said, 'you're a good actor.'

'Thank you, but no, not me. I'll be one of the roadies. I'll be in charge of stage lighting,' he said as he threw a couple of hunks of wood on the fire, 'and drinks.'

I said, 'Kylie, here read this out,' and I handed her a sheet of paper.

'What is it?'

'Just read it out. You're not to look at it first, okay?'

'All right, I trust you, but I don't know why. Your track record isn't so hot.'

'Ye of little respect.'

The others were yarning and to get their attention Kylie announced loudly, 'Okay you lot. Dad wants me to read this to you. I can't tell you what it is because I don't know, and I can't see anyway.'

'Come over here nearer the light.'

'Okay. Here goes. It's called, "The Real Identity of the Snowy River Rider".

There's a good reason to think we're on the brink
Of something bigger than big.
Perhaps the rider could have been an outsider
Who just joined in for the gig.

Kylie stopped, 'Dad, who wrote this?'

'Just read it. You'll find out.'

No one knew the name of each who was game
Prepared for the ride of their life.
So they all assumed – shouldn't have presumed
The rider couldn't be a man's wife.

A skinny grey mount, so many years lost count
Looked like it should have been dead.

It might have thrown a shoe or maybe even two
No matter when given its head.

Blew them out of the water she shouldna oughta
They paled when she took off her hat.
Grudging but impressed their shock they expressed
How could they ever acknowledge that?

'Here, what's this on the bottom? Hop out of the light, Dad. It's small writing. *"Written by Banjo Winn"*,' she read.

'When did you write that?' Karyn asked. 'I've never heard it before.'

'Just this afternoon, down by the water. I didn't know Rob was going to do the real thing.'

'Well you're a dark horse, aren't you?' Mick said.

'Three parts thoroughbred at least.'

'The other part leaves a bit to be desired, though,' Karyn jibed.

'True, I feel like a busted-arse carthorse some mornings. All right, who's next? Who can sing?' I kept on.

No volunteers.

'What's your favourite song, Kylie? Have you and Mick got your own theme song?' I asked.

'Yeah, but I'm not telling you. Some things are private.'

'What about your second choice then?'

'Hmmm, "Sweet Jane", by the Cowboy Junkies.'

'Have you got one, Dan?'

'I can't sing it, but I can put it on if you want,' he offered.

'Shit no. We'll leave Lee Kernaghan for another day. Thanks anyway mate.'

'What about you two?' Rob asked Karyn and me.

'"Stranger on the Shore",' we answered simultaneously, 'and no, we're not telling why.'

'Better not to know,' Kylie said, 'we might end up with too much information.'

'Yeah, that could be the case,' I smiled at Karyn, then winked, and even in the half-light and after thirty years of marriage I swear I saw her blush.

Kylie continued, 'What about you, Rob? Anything special?'

'Mmmm . . . yes, and it's got a bit of a story to it. Tell you when I get back. Nature calls.'

'Anybody want another drink while I'm up?' asked Mick the roadie.

'Top the kettle up for coffee please,' Kylie said.

He did so and stoked the fire while he was at it. The conversation died momentarily as we sat gazing into the eager new flames.

'What's that?' Karyn asked, leaning forward on her chair and listening intently.

'What's what?'

'That sound, coming from down along the shore. I'd swear it's a clarinet. Listen.'

'Somebody playing "Stranger on the Shore", that's what it is,' I said.

'Where's Rob?' Kylie looked around, puzzled. 'It's got to be him.'

At first the notes echoed softly across the moonlit lake, then slowly became clearer. The familiar lament seeped into my soul and took control, transporting me to a higher plane and another time. I looked over at Karyn and she appeared equally moved. Eventually the firelight picked up a shadowy movement and slowly Rob materialised into the ring of light, finishing the most touching rendition of our theme song. Its sad, final note hung in the air.

Magic. Karyn's face was now streaming tears as she threw her arms around my neck. I tried to blink back my tears and failed. Kylie fished in her jeans pocket for a tissue and simultaneously the boys felt the urgent need to have a pee. I think Rob may have had a tear in his eye as well – perhaps seeing the effect his music had on us.

When she could talk, Karyn said, 'Rob, that was out of this world. It was just so . . . beautiful. Thank you.'

I was blown away. 'Christ, mate, how and when did you learn to play like that? That was better than Acker Bilk.'

'Should be. I taught him.'

'How bloody old are you? You hold it well,' I laughed.

'Geez, Rob, what else have you got up your sleeve?' Dan said.

'Nothing. I think it's coffee time. Am I too late?'

Mick answered, 'No, not at all. I forgot about it when you played your solo number. I'll get right onto it.'

'What a concert. Pity it has to come to an end. I've never enjoyed anything so much in all my life,' Karyn said and Kylie nodded in agreement.

'Sorry I don't know "Sweet Jane", Kylie,' Rob said. 'It would have been nice to play it for you.'

'What I've heard tonight will keep me going, Rob. Thank you so much. It's been marvellous.'

The coffee dispensed with, the party seemed at an end.

'I don't know about you, Rob,' Mick remarked. 'What should we call you? Banjo? Clancy? Acker? Who next?'

'I reckon Stranger on the Shore would fit pretty well,' I suggested.

An idea to which everyone agreed.

'Well, how about you let this Stranger do one last number for you?'

We all looked at each other, not knowing what to think as Rob disappeared into the darkness once again.

He was away only a minute, and returned with a carpenter's saw in one hand and violin bow in the other. I'd heard a recording of a musical saw, but had never seen a performance. On closer inspection I noticed that the saw had no teeth.

'Mate, do they make these especially for musicians?' I asked.

'No. Not really. All you have to do is order a blank from the factory. Music stores probably wouldn't sell many.'

He constantly altered the tension on the saw blade by buckling it and in conjunction with the bow being drawn across the spine produced a whole range of quavering notes. For a few moments he seemed to tune it. Then, making himself comfortable he proceeded with a very different kind of music, at once soulful and disturbing. The haunting sound of Rob's last piece was answered by a lone dingo, whose moonlight howl brought up the hairs on our necks.

Rob bowed, 'On that note I bid you all goodnight.'

Many months later, Bradley Murdoch was apprehended in connection with the Peter Falconio – Joanne Lees case. In due course he was convicted of Peter's murder, although a body was never found. Joanne returned to her home in England. I couldn't help wondering how different things would have been for those young kids if they'd met Rob Hughes in the outback instead.

LEIGH HENZELL
Set in stone

———◆———

'**I**'ve made up my mind. I'm going to build a church,' Leigh announced one night in the Crown Hotel.

Every Thursday evening, by evolution rather than design, a large group of our friends gathered at the Crown. It was the focal point of our tiny community, and Leigh and his wife Lynette were its hosts. Built in 1913, Leigh's old wooden pub stands as a relic of long-forgotten times. The hitching rail at the front is a reminder of times when patient horses dozed while their drunken riders boozed. Four weeping figs supported by ever-spreading cathedral buttresses shade the sweeping verandahs – a cool retreat in a subtropical climate.

I don't know what publicans are supposed to look like, but Leigh doesn't look like one to me. His face is lean, lined and weathered and it's rare to see him in anything but a khaki shirt and shorts and Blundstone work boots. If publicans are supposed to have bloated faces and lumpy, purple-red noses from the booze, well, he doesn't fit the mould. His straight thinnish nose bears the stamp of Continental blood. Nothing about him fits any mould.

'Build a church? I didn't know you were religious mate,' I said. But I knew the family. I didn't really need to point this out.

'I'm not. This is nothing to do with religion. Our family lost its homeland because of bloody religion long before they ever migrated to Australia.'

Heads turned. Ears pricked. Nobody spoke.

'Yep, I'm starting as soon as possible.'

We were used to Leigh's schemes, and to his storytelling ability. I shouldn't have been surprised.

I recalled the many Easter holiday breaks we took together at a nearby 2000-acre mountain property – perhaps a dozen families in all. And every year, for the past fifteen, Leigh continued a story-telling tradition. 'All right you kids, come over here near the camp fire and I'll tell you about how Mrs McMurtry fell down the well,' Leigh said one Easter, winking at any adult nearby. Kids of all sizes love him.

They didn't take much mustering. Little ones looked bewildered as they were dragged along by slightly bigger ones, who looked at each other knowingly. Teenagers sighed deeply, but came to listen anyway. One of the fathers always said, 'Don't start till I get another stubby.'

The story had been going on for fifteen years now and poor bloody Mrs Mac was still in the well.

'Uncle Leigh, what actually happens to Mrs McMurtry? Does she drown or does she get out? We're going to live in Canberra, so I won't be here next year to find out.'

'You don't have to be here next year. Come back in five years. You might find out, then again you mightn't.'

Still nobody had responded to Leigh's revelation of his intention to build a church. No one knew what to say. Quizzical expressions probably said enough.

Typical Leigh – drop a clanger into the conversation, then disappear out of the bistro and into the public bar to continue supervising the evening's trading.

'Is he fair dinkum, Lynette?' somebody asked.

'You know what he's like. If he's made up his mind then it will happen. He's been talking about it for a long while.'

'I didn't know he was religious,' again I fished about for an explanation.

'This is nothing to do with religion,' she echoed.

Best leave well alone, I thought.

Soon after, and once again on a Thursday night, he disclosed that he was going to build the church on the farm.

'Not in the middle of a pineapple patch surely, Leigh?' a somewhat religious friend joked.

'No. The thought of the rough end of a pineapple, and where it is usually advised to be jammed, might put some people off.'

'That leaves the home farm – the dairy farm, I take it,' the friend continued, perhaps amused (or offended) at the pineapple patch suggestion.

'Yes. Down below where the old swimming pool was and over towards the old man's house a bit. I've got it all pegged.'

'There's no doubt about it then?' I asked.

'No, why? I told you a little while back. Why would you think that?'

No reason.

'It won't be a normal church either.'

I looked towards him, inviting him to say more.

'It'll really be a chapel, for a start anyway. I might go further with it later.'

'Oh —'

'I'll have it finished for Leanne's wedding.'

'A big job, mate. You haven't got that long.'

'No, that's right,' he said, and hurried off.

'When we were on our honeymoon we saw a little chapel on a property down in the Hunter Valley,' Lynette explained later. 'God, how long ago was that? Must be, er, too many years. Early '60s we got married. Leigh has never forgotten about it. He said then that he'd build something like it later for our family.'

'What did you think?'

'Not much. I told him we'd better get some kids first.'

I had called into the Crown one afternoon during the week, and as usual the topic of Leigh's project came up. Discussing it was a welcome break from the usual politics and cricket Test scores.

'He doesn't practise any religion as far as I can see,' a friend said.

'It's not a church. It's a chapel,' I defended. 'And Leigh doesn't practise any religion that I know of either, but he does live by Christian principles. You'd have to agree, wouldn't you?'

A nod of grudging agreement.

'Leigh tells me it'll be for everybody. They can "bring their own religion with them", he says.'

I went on, 'It'll just be a country chapel. There's a lot of good in Leigh, you know.'

'Yeah, I'm not saying there isn't.'

'He practises what he preaches, for want of a better way of putting it,' I added.

'Sometimes we mightn't like what he preaches, but he does practise it,' an eavesdropper interrupted.

I stepped back to include the newcomer in the conversation and continued.

'Who else would take on some employees who might find it hard to get a job anywhere else? And not just one or two of them either. I don't know of many others who'd do that.'

'Yeah, he does. But don't you worry; he gets his pound of flesh out of them. You know what pineapple work is like.' My friend's drink was at risk as he gestured in emphasis.

'I know they have to work hard, but they get bloody well treated.' I was getting a bit hot under the collar. 'He doesn't work them any harder than he works himself. Anyway, hard work never killed anybody.'

The conversation was going nowhere and we all knew it, so we let the matter drop.

I thought about Leigh's employees. I knew that in addition to their annual four weeks' holiday, every year Leigh says, 'All right you blokes, we leave on Friday morning. All you'll need is your clothes. I'll fix the rest,' and he takes them on a fishing trip to Fraser Island or Double Island Point for a week or so, all expenses paid. Everything. They don't even need their wallets. That has gone on for years and continues to this day.

His latest incarnation was the biggest thing to happen in our community for many years. Tongues were wagging. Comment was not always supportive. And Leigh didn't bat an eyelid.

Work began at a brisk pace. Our family was involved with the project in small ways. An ironbark log had been sourced from Leigh's pineapple farm wasteland and had been milled into a rectangular shape to be used as a lintel over the main entrance to the chapel. The heavy girder was delivered to our workshop and I was asked to arrange the inscription on it. We had the heavy lifting gear to handle the job and I knew the right craftsman for the carving.

Other times, through our business, we supplied small amounts of materials on site. Occasionally I turned up out of interest, and it was at those times that I gained a good insight into Leigh's thoughts about the project. He seemed to welcome the company while he was working. Or maybe I actually got in the way and he was too polite to say so.

'I'll have to find a stonemason. I'm building it out of stone from the Boral pit,' he said.

The quarry is only 6 kilometres out of town. The blue rock is blasted out, crushed, and most often sold as road base. But for orders like Leigh's, they used the front-end loader and tipped some of the blasted rock over a 12-inch screen before it went into the big crushers. Any pieces that fell through were suitable for projects such as his. Many people used this material for retaining walls. Procuring it wasn't a problem, but there wasn't a stonemason in the district who would take on a project on the scale of Leigh's chapel. He searched high and low.

'Never thought it would be this hard,' he said.

Finally he did find a man, John Austin, an Englishman – no, a Cornishman. He was a stonemason by trade and turned out to be just the man for the job. He plied his trade in the adjacent district, only 20 kilometres away. Work now started in earnest.

'I want the building to be perfectly aligned north–south. All great cathedrals are.'

Who were we to doubt it? Cathedral indeed! Had his imagination taken over?

'And it's got to be true to the Greenwich line, not magnetic north.'

He'd done his homework, as usual.

'If it's possible I want it to be able to pick up the sun through slots in the wall to capture the summer and winter solstice, just like they did at Stonehenge.'

How did Leigh know anything about Stonehenge? I didn't.

'This might leave St John's Cathedral in Brisbane for dead, Leigh,' I joked.

'Bit smaller, but just as much character – probably more.' He wasn't joking.

I said, 'Do you know that St John's has taken a hundred years to get this far and it's nowhere near finished yet? I know that's true because they've just been onto Mum for a subscription.'

He wasn't fazed. 'I haven't got much more than a hundred days to finish this.'

The place was soon a hive of industry – backhoes and trenchers, reinforcing mesh and bolt cutters, cement trucks and concrete pumps, council inspectors who'd never presided over this sort of building before.

'Have a bit of imagination you blokes. Does this look like it's going to fall over?'

And common sense did prevail.

As I arrived on site one morning Leigh was busy sorting likely rocks for the mason from the scattered pile nearby.

'How'yer goin'?' I asked. 'Christ, you've got a go-on since I was here last. Your stone man knows his job by the looks.'

'Yeah, slow getting a start but we're away now. We had to stop and have a family ceremony for laying the foundation stone. I'll show you a photo of it. Real important that was,' he laughed, but I knew he was serious.

The wheelbarrow looked half-full but it was loaded. As he went off to empty it near the pile of brickie's loam he wobbled about a bit with the weight, which he'd underestimated. He's wiry and strong but not a heavy man.

The day was warming up and I said to him, 'Where's your hat mate? You'll get bloody skin cancer.'

'Boils your brains,' he said – the standard reply.

'You used to wear a hat a lot then, eh?' I suggested with a

smart-arse smile. The comment didn't warrant an answer. Surprisingly, I've never seen him sunburnt, although he doesn't have an olive complexion.

'They sell this stuff by the ton. There's half a ton in this barrow. They must make a fortune.'

He paused, then went on, 'There's a hell of a lot of work before you see much for it. John's missus comes and helps most days. She usually does what I'm doing.'

'Leigh, isn't this a huge expense to go to for Leanne's wedding and the odd family function?'

'Well, yes. But life's been pretty good to me you know. I'd like the same for everybody. Good parents who got me started, good marriage, good kids. You know some poor buggers can only dream about the lifestyle we lead. It's time I put a little bit back. I don't know if this will make any difference, but it will to me.'

As if contemplating what he'd just said, he went quiet for a few moments.

'Yes, it is a lot of money and you know what a terrible miserable bugger I am,' he laughed, 'but this is important. It's one of the most important things I'll ever do in my life. You know it's not just for my family. Your kids might want to use it one day. It'll be here a long time. Your grandkids could even use it.'

I'd heard him say often enough that he had long pockets and short arms, but what he said and what he did, well, they didn't stack up. He reckoned he got his so-called miserly streak from his Scottish ancestry.

I thought about that. It didn't ring true.

'Leigh, I always thought your ancestry was Austrian.'

'Yes, it is, on the Henzell side. But they ended up in France because of religious persecution. The Scottish bit is from Mum.'

'Oh, okay. I thought I remembered you saying they were Austrian glassblowers.'

'Yeah, that's nearly right. Not glassblowers, glass manufacturers. They were very welcome in France with that technology. They were treated like royalty. Skilled tradesmen became blue bloods. You don't read much of that sort of thing in the history books, do you? It was the French who designed our coat of arms and awarded it to our ancestors.'

'When?'

'Geez I don't know. Bloody long time ago. There might have been an earlier one in Austria, but apparently all was lost. On the other hand, mind you, it was the Scottish part that prompted me to buy the pub to get some of my own money back.' He winked.

'What – from glassmaker to glass polisher?'

'No, to glass filler. Bit of a difference if I'd gone from glassmaker to glass emptier.'

'Nothing's changed there has it?' I ask. 'You still empty quite a few glasses.'

'Yeah. Be a damn shame if that ever came to an end.'

We laughed about that.

Leigh took a plan from his ute and went over to one of the tradesmen who was up on a scaffold. After a lot of arm waving and map re-orientation, he returned.

'Geez he's a bloody good lad, that young Ronnie. Knows what he's doing. Half the time I've got the bloody plan upside down.'

'Bullshit.'

'Well, once I did.'

'You're allowed once.'

'Just while I think of it, I'd better come round to your place and get that inscription started. We won't have the luxury of making even one mistake on it.'

'No, we'll measure it all and pencil the letters in where they should be – so long as we can spell. I'll get you to approve it before we put a chisel into it,' I said. 'Then any mistake won't be mine.'

'How about we do it now and then you can get onto it straightaway. We'll need it soon, before the roof goes on.'

And so we did.

'I'll bring it around on the crane truck as soon as it's finished if you want.'

'No, I'll come and get it, if you'll load it on my truck. Be a bugger to have to lift it twice. It might have to stay on my truck for a week. You never know.'

That made sense.

A little while later he said, 'I heard that there's a rumour going round that I'm building a monument to myself.'

'I heard that too. Hardly worry you, would it?'

'Doesn't worry me at all. But it hurts a bit. No, it doesn't hurt, it saddens me. Some poor buggers have got nothing better to do than criticise. I can guess who started it. He hasn't got much between the ears. Might have even missed out completely,' he laughed.

And I would have expected that from Leigh. His sense of humour always kept him buoyed. His total focus on the job at hand hardly gave him time to dwell on such trivia. Focus was his forté – a driven man with the courage of his convictions.

A fortnight later we were in the pub for our regular Thursday night sojourn. During the evening we'd reverted to conversation about Leigh's project. What else? His passion had never waned.

'You know, our society is falling apart. You've only got to look around you. Look at what's happening. Kids have no respect, but it's not their fault, it's the damn parents – or parent. And there's another thing. The bloody government encourages kids to leave their families – pays them almost, giving them a wage to stay away when they should be trying to get them back home.'

He continued, on a roll now. 'You know, if your family pulls together there's nothing in this world you can't do, nothing you can't achieve. I don't know if I can make any difference with this little chapel, but if somehow I can make it a family thing, well, I'll be real pleased.'

As work continued at a cracking pace, Leigh and Lynette busily sourced the finishing touches – a bible from England, leadlights, pews, a font. Then, just two weeks before Leanne and Peter's wedding the chapel was complete in every detail.

Bouquets on road signs and tied to tree trunks marked the way for the 8 kilometres from Dayboro township.

'No chance of getting lost,' I said to Karyn, as we turned into the Henzells' place. A couple of lofty blue gums towered on either side of the gateway – not planted, but preserved. They stood as survivor sentinels, saved from the logger's crosscut saw a century ago. Somebody cared then – Leigh's grandfather, old Gurney, probably. And now Leigh does.

The laneway access to the Henzell dairy farm branched off Mt Pleasant Road dissecting a neighbour's cultivation paddock, seasonally planted with ryegrass in winter or left fallow in summer with a disorderly profusion of native species. Such contrasting images: English-irrigated green; Aussie dry-spell brown. Tired grey fence posts barely supported their sagging barbwire, rusted now but still adequate to keep the neighbour's docile milkers in check. Where there was less sunlight, on the southern side of the posts, scalloped cookie-cutter fungi struggled to survive.

Then, the lane dipped out of sight to a concrete creek crossing before re-emerging and forking – left to the dairy, right to the homestead.

'Be bloody lucky to get a park. Look at this lot,' I said, taking the right fork.

'Lynette said they were coming from everywhere. England, Papua New Guinea, the States . . .'

'We live bloody near next door and it looks like the whole lot beat us here.'

'Well it's a pretty important occasion, their only daughter getting married.'

Springtime. A full carpet of jacaranda blossoms – glorious. Above, a mighty umbrella of lavender shaded the wedding guests as they chattered excitedly. A breathtaking setting – all created by a single tree and a manicured lawn. At the slightest breeze bell-shaped flowers rained down on the white marquee.

Women in their finery, wearing the very best they could buy. Men in their penguin suits wearing the very best they could hire – they matched the Friesian heifers nearby, and didn't look nearly as comfortable. Greetings, smeared lipstick on cheeks, air kisses . . . mwuh-mwuh!

'Love your dress, where did you get it?' one friend asked another, deftly turning the collar to observe.

'It's Target's new label,' came the answer, pronounced Tar-*zhay*.

'Have you got any grandkids yet?' another asked.

'Yes, three. Have any of your kids got started?'

'Geez, hasn't Alec put on weight?' somebody observed.

'Have you ever seen what they eat?'

Suddenly Alec's wife joined them and they froze. She said, 'Don't look now, but hasn't Gloria aged since she lost all that weight.'

They relaxed.

Another said, 'I think Gloria's taken the diet too far. It doesn't suit her being so skinny. You'll have to get her to have a talk to Alec.'

'Mmm,' said Alec's wife. *Bitch*.

G'days, handshakes all round. Friggin' hot for this time of year.

'You look well, Alec.'

'Too well. This bloody suit's shrunk,' he frowned concern, but smiled.

'Dry isn't it?'

'My oath, too bloody dry,' answered a bloke from the Darling Downs.

'Setting up the bar, I see,' Alec noticed.

'Bloody good thing that.'

The forty seats in the chapel had been reserved, the two front rows for family – mother of the bride, a space for Leigh, and the rest of the close family and in-laws in order. Lynette tried to smile at relatives as they were ushered to their seats, but her expression transformed into tears of joy. She rectified the makeup damage by careful dabbing under her eyes, one then the other.

The older folk, and other women who would want to cry, occupied the rest of the seats. Perhaps another hundred stood outside and formed an 'aisle' across the lavender flowers and onto the red carpet that was rolled out across the lawn.

Then 'here comes the bride', right on time. Leanne looked beautiful – radiant, happy – walking slowly, arm in arm with her father. Leigh's smile took up most of his face.

A hush descended. A string quartet, led by a cousin of the groom, had been playing softly and faded – Mozart's piece replaced by Pachelbel's Canon.

Leanne wore a stunning cream off-the-shoulder gown and was attended by a flower girl and two bridesmaids. At the chapel entrance she paused, smiled at her father and squeezed his arm, then together they walked the short distance down the chapel aisle. She took her place beside her future husband, and Peter turned to face her.

Leigh's cousin, the Reverend Bruce Henzell, officiated.

'Do you take this woman . . . wedded wife . . . Mr and Mrs Dalton.'

And so the chapel witnessed its first wedding.

As husband and wife emerged the bell tolled and the crowd clapped and whistled in a rising crescendo. Three heifers took off down the paddock in fright, but then changed their minds, bucked and kicked their heels high. Obviously they were delighted too.

'Leigh, have you trained those heifers?' I asked.

'Yes. Took a while. Had to go through half the herd and two auditions before I got what I wanted, but it was all worth it, don't you reckon?'

Kisses, hugs, handshakes and photos for the couple, laughter, chatter, champagne and beer for the crowd. Alec took his coat off, loosened his tie and let his belt out a notch. Darcy Condon told Roy Kanowski and me a most improbable story about a rabbit with a half stick of gelignite blowing up a Landcruiser. Howard Spark told another story about what a terrible lying bastard Darcy was. And Darcy said that Howard wouldn't know because he wasn't there. Howard said that he didn't have to be.

The scene was set for a wonderful evening in the huge marquee nearby.

For Leigh it was a dream realised.

The following winter, I stood alone under the leafless skeleton of the jacaranda and looked northward, imagining how Leigh had dreamed of the chapel. The chill seemed fitting for my visit – a different perspective. Something prompted me to look upward. I followed the branch above me along to the nest of a tawny frogmouth. She would breed again in the spring. I wondered how long frogmouths lived.

Sombre grey clouds seemed to descend through the mist to touch the damp slate roof of the little chapel, which sat shrouded, tucked into the hillside as if it had been there for a century. It would look the same in another hundred years.

Treading carefully down the five stone steps into the chapel I noticed the bell above the entrance awaiting the next celebration.

My eyes travelled over the two heavy doors, closed and cold, and I focused on the heavy lintel above. There inscribed were the words, 'Lord I pray you take care of my life'. These formal, family words were passed down through many generations. I helped to put them there, and felt proud to have done so. The building was not locked – it never is – and I lifted the solid latch.

Stepping into the aisle, I tried to focus in the gloom. I was drawn to the cross-shaped light high in the wall, created by slots in the stonework. Another slot was supposed to catch both the summer and winter solstices – those points in time when the sun appears to pause before resuming its elliptical journey – but it wasn't to be because the wall was too thick. Perhaps the only disappointment.

A stained-glass window in the back wall, under the cross, added a little to the feeble light. The coat of arms mounted alongside bore the inscription *Seigneur je te prie garde ma vie* (Lord I pray you take care of my life).

On that day, the chapel was soulful and brooding.

The following day it would witness the funeral of a dear friend. And the day after that it was booked for a wedding.

One man's dream. All welcome – no charge.

At Christmas of that year, a large group of friends and family and all their children gathered at the chapel for Carols by Candlelight – the men with their eskies for sustenance.

'Just as well I never got it consecrated,' Leigh said laughing, 'otherwise we would have to sing our carols through the window from the outside.'

'Only the kids would have been allowed in,' somebody said.

'Yeah,' Leigh agreed.

As the night wore on and the gathering around the piano grew bigger and finer in voice Lynette was heard to say, 'Be careful there! Don't knock that urn over, or you'll have Leigh's parents all over the keyboard.'

The party missed a beat, or two.

'Do you think your parents would approve, Leigh?' one of the men asked.

'What, being spread over the keyboard? I don't think so.'

'Hell no, mate. I meant of the chapel and the carols.'

'I thought you were going to say "of the eskies". Yeah, of course they would. It's all about families, isn't it? That's the main thing. Do you think all of these kids would have gone to another church to sing carols with their parents on Christmas Eve? Teenagers, little kids, all sizes? Not likely, mate.'

Later, after many carol renditions and generous expressions of 'goodwill towards men', the parents of little ones headed homeward. A few of us with no Santa obligations sat in the back pew reflecting on the evening.

'Leigh, this place is beautiful. But it's more than that,' Karyn said. 'I feel something different here. *I* feel different here.'

'Yeah. Depends what's happening.'

'You've created that, Leigh. It's a pretty big thing to achieve,' Karyn added.

I said, 'It's starting to be important in many people's lives, and not just in our community either.'

'I hadn't thought of it like that before,' said Leigh. 'You might be right. I'd love to think so.'

'I reckon it transcends any religion. All faiths are welcome here. You're a true visionary, Leigh.'

'Thank you, my friend.'

'DOLLY' LEIS
As years go by

———•◆•———

Peter and I were both struggling awkwardly up the stockyard rails when Dolly put her left hand on the top rung of the steel gate beside us, her left foot on the second-bottom rung and swung easily over the top, then put the right foot on the same rung from the other side and dropped down lightly. Peter and I looked at each other in surprise. I felt a bit inadequate, and I could tell by his expression that he did too. Dolly didn't look back as she walked off briskly in her gumboots, skirts swinging, clamping her old rag hat down more firmly on her head as a gust of wind threatened to snatch it away. She didn't witness us touch down heavily. Dolly is Peter's mother.

'Shit, Peter, I'm glad she didn't see us pair of useless bastards. I thought I was in pretty good nick till a moment ago.'

'Yeah, she keeps herself fit, the old girl. I keep telling her to slow down a bit.'

'Does she still go down to the bails early? I often see your bike light about three o'clock when you go for the cows.'

'No, Mum sleeps in a bit these days, but she still comes down a lot of mornings. I haven't got a hope of stopping her. Not that I'd want to. She's still better in the dairy than any workman we've ever had. Good with the youngsters too.'

'Yeah, I see her over there at the calf pens sometimes when they're being fed, always talking to them and petting them.'

'She keeps on even as they grow into heifers. That way when we have to break them into the milking shed she already knows every one of them. She generally knows the ones that are likely to be trouble. It helps a lot. They recognise her voice and know she's gentle. You know women are usually better in the dairy than men.'

I nodded. I'd have to agree with that.

I had called into Leis' dairy and the three of us had been helping a Friesian heifer with a very difficult birth. When I arrived, about six inches of the unborn calf's front legs were protruding and that's where both lives would have ended without human intervention.

The Leis' herd was regarded as one of the best commercial herds in south-east Queensland and this heifer was perhaps worth the equivalent of three weeks' wages for an ordinary working man. So she was worth saving in terms of dollars, and worth saving in terms of sentiment, too.

'Peter,' Dolly said, 'I think the calf's head is facing backwards. It'll never come out like this. You'll have to turn it if you can.'

'Yeah, Ma, I know. I hate this job.'

'She'll die . . . both of them will.'

Peter struggled between the heifer's contractions to get one hand in far enough to pull the head around.

'If my arms weren't so bloody thick it'd help. You might have more chance,' he said to his mother.

Dolly nodded. She got down on her knees beside the groaning mother-to-be, waited till the heifer's immediate contraction was over and tried to slide her arm in.

'You poor little thing. Let's see what we can do.'

Dolly failed on her first attempt, so changed her position and with her left hand on the heifer's hip for leverage tried again to slide her hand in. The second attempt was also unsuccessful. After the stressed heifer's next wave of even stronger contractions had subsided, Dolly braced herself and tried again. This time with extreme effort she eventually pushed the calf back in a few centimetres to give her room to turn the head. The calf's nose was now exposed. Puffing from the exertion Dolly rose and patted the heifer. 'You'll be right girl,' she said, and stood back for Peter to take over.

Peter fixed a purpose-built puller to the calf's feet and strained hard to encourage the birth. The legs came part way and the head was half born, but the calf refused to come any further.

'Here, Rhylle, get on this with me and pull like hell – with the contractions.'

Two of us, both about ninety kilos, used all of our strength, but barely budged the head. Then the calf came quickly, but only to the shoulders. The baby's tongue was blue – not a good sign. It wouldn't last much longer. The shoulders lodged in the same manner as the head, but then, in the same way, eventually came free too. The rest of the body came easily. Another live birth – another heifer saved.

'That's one way to cut down on vet's bills,' I said.

'Yeah, damn vets are too dear,' Dolly replied, 'and you can't get them when you want them. They don't know as much as Peter anyway.'

'Dunno, Mum. You've been around cows a long while.'

'Well, animals aren't that different from people. I've had five kids so I should know a bit about this part of it,' she said matter-of-factly. 'Anyway, we can't do much more here. She should be on her feet pretty soon. I'll come back and check her later.'

We've just saved a life, no two lives, I thought, *and Dolly doesn't even see it as anything out of the ordinary.*

The Leis farm is 3 kilometres from Dayboro in south-east Queensland. I cast my mind back to Dolly's home town in the 1950s, when I first knew it. The hotel sat at one end of the main street, the old butter factory at the other, with the butcher and baker vying for the middle ground. Four churches, the secret order of the masons and a school way up on the hill completed the picture. There was a post office too, and other buildings that I can't quite recall. No new homes had been built for many years and the old ones gave the place a quaint charm. Actually, Dayboro isn't much different today from what it was in 1955, or even 1920 when Dolly was a toddler. Not much different at all apart from the twenty-odd real estate agents who've discovered our secret backwater.

The 300-acre farm is in the prized King Scrub locality, named because it literally was a 'king scrub'. Red cedar, beech, quandong, satinwood and more grew there prolifically in the early days, and after logging, clearing and burning, high quality brown soil was exposed – ideal for dairying.

Driving home a week or so after the episode with the calf, I spotted my neighbour walking along the side of the road.

'Do you want a lift, Dolly?' I asked as I pulled up beside her. She had her basket on her arm, heavy with her purchases. The answer was predictable, but still I offered. I always felt compelled to ask just in case she accepted.

'No thanks, Rhylle. I need the exercise. Thanks for stopping,' she said and continued on her way.

She walks to Dayboro township regularly. It's all downhill so it's easy – too easy, she says, so she walks back up the winding mountain road to make it worthwhile.

As I drove off, she slowed and turned towards my car, shading her eyes under her little straw hat, and gave a friendly wave. While her face shows the character of a lifetime of work and exposure to the sun, when Dolly goes to town, with her lipstick on, her soft white hair framing her face, and a wonderful smile, she could easily pass for a woman fifteen years younger.

Seeing her on the road that day prompted a thought. I'd known her for a long time, but I'd never *really* sat down and talked to her. We'd only ever had brief though pleasant conversations, usually about a current event – like the birth of that calf – and they'd never gone much further. I realised that I knew a lot about her, but did not really know her. She lived in the big house on her own since her husband died and her family left home. She might enjoy a talk. So I asked.

'I haven't got a story,' she said, 'I've only ever been here, milking cows.'

'There're a lot of people in this world who would have absolutely no idea about life on a dairy. Could we talk about it?'

'I suppose,' she laughed, 'it can't do any harm. You already know everything about me.'

I said, 'Just pretend I'm a stranger.'

'I'd be shy with a stranger,' she said almost coyly. 'I wouldn't know what to say.'

'Come on, will you do it?'

'Well, all right.'

'I don't want to rush you, but could we get started fairly soon?' I asked. 'Like, this afternoon?'

'All right. I'm not going to the bails,' she answered.

So I went back midafternoon.

'Where will we start?' she said, 'Would you like a cup of tea or will we wait for later?'

'Later, eh? Might need it more then.'

'Rhylle, you sit here.' She indicated a cane chair, then made herself comfortable on a similar one by the verandah rail. I guessed it might have been a favourable spot. She looked at me expectantly.

'I know "Dolly" is your nickname —'

'I don't recall anyone ever calling me anything else,' she answered quickly.

I thought she might volunteer her real name. When she didn't it was on the tip of my tongue to ask but I changed my mind at the last minute, thinking that such a question could be an invasion of privacy. I suppose it could have been 'Doris', but I didn't really need to know – Dolly suited her so well. Instead I asked, 'Dolly were you dairying here when you were first married?'

'Yeah, for a good while before Bev was born and she's older than Peter and he's not far off sixty.'

'What? All those years?'

'There was never anywhere else I wanted to go or anything else I wanted to do.'

I shook my head, taking that in. 'Has it ever bothered you having the house in the middle of all the farm buildings? You'd never be able to leave your work behind would you?'

'No, I like it. You always know what's going on. The brewery grain and pineapple waste get a bit smelly sometimes, but you get used to that. I don't even notice it.'

'When they built the maternity yard for the calving cows did they deliberately site it under your bedroom window?'

'Yes, I'm sure. But Ony reckoned it was the only place he could put it. When I said "over near the barn" he didn't seem to hear.' She smiled as she said this, the anecdote probably stirring up other long-forgotten memories of her husband.

'How long ago did he build it?'

'A fair while before he died. He's been gone more than twenty years.'

'It's pretty handy for you to supervise the births, isn't it?' I suggest.

'Yes. All day and all night.'

During the night Dolly had witnessed another birth, an easy, natural one this time. There were plenty of them with 150 milkers in the herd and another thirty or so heifers coming on at any one time.

The maternity ward was floodlit. Sometimes Dolly was up three or four times a night checking on the progress of several births.

'A few months ago I asked Peter if he was letting those heifers go in calf too early – there were too many having a tough time of it,' she told me. 'He said he thought it was more to do with that boofheaded Hereford bull throwing big calves. He's going to put a little Jersey in with the heifers. Be good to get a Jersey and lift the butterfat a bit.'

'Is the butterfat a problem?'

'No, not for whole milk to go into the supermarkets, but we produce a lot of over-quota milk for cheese making and yoghurt – that's where butterfat counts. We win the milk quality competition at the show nearly every year, you know.'

'That says something, doesn't it?'

'Yeah, Peter's one of the best dairymen in Queensland. He selects all the best bulls from the AI catalogue and does all the artificial insemination. And you know he does a lot of the vet work – you've seen that.'

'He knows what he's on about, eh?'

'Yes, he does. He really does,' she beamed.

'Do you ever get bored, Dolly, with every day the same?' I asked.

'No, there's always something going on. The only part that's the same is the milking.'

'You don't mind the routine, then?'

'It's good for you. It's good to have a routine, and I can still get around pretty well. I'm happy even though I'm getting a bit old.'

A *bit* old, I thought, smiling to myself.

'I've been lucky,' Dolly continued. 'The girls come fairly often and I've got Peter and Nerida and their kids just across the road. And I've got my drawing. Do you want to see some of it?'

I nodded and before I could answer she hopped straight up and disappeared down the hallway. She returned with a far-from-amateurish colour sketch of a pair of rainbow lorikeets feeding on nectar from the flowers of a grevillea.

'Dolly, that's good.'

'It's not finished yet.'

'I'm impressed.'

'I'm not happy with the one that's hanging upside down. I turned the board up the other way to do him, and now he just looks like he's standing on his head.'

'You're a bit hard on yourself. He looks pretty good to me.'

'No, I've got to fix him,' she said matter-of-factly. She slid the drawing down beside her so that it leant against the chair leg, and that seemed the end of the artwork conversation.

While I'd been waiting for her to return I'd been taking note of the volume of traffic zooming by. Since the road had been made into a tourist drive a few years ago, traffic had increased tenfold.

'This is like Queen Street! Does the traffic worry you when you're crossing the cows over?'

'We've never had an accident – yet, cross your fingers. Hope we never do. We did have a funny thing happen a few years ago, though.' She chuckled. 'Peter and I were bringing the cows in for the afternoon milking and this bloke came tearing along.'

I knew what she meant by afternoon milking. It meant one o'clock, every day, right on the knocker. The cows have to walk from the 'day' paddock across the main road leading to Mt Mee. Usually all traffic stops as the cows, udders full and swinging, make their way across the bitumen to the milking shed.

She went on, 'He was going so fast I thought he'd never stop. He nearly didn't. Then he tried to go barging through in his little battered car almost on top of the cows. Peter yelled at him and told him he'd see to him if he hit one of them.'

'What did the bloke do?'

'He was real stirred up he was, shouting, blowing the horn and carrying on. Peter went over to him with the whip in his hand, but even that didn't make any difference.'

'He didn't hit any did he?'

'He bumped a couple of the old milkers, but not hard. He was real wild-looking. When he got through he took off, revving up, skidding everywhere in the cowshit, all over the place, off into the gutter, half up the bank. His wheels wouldn't grip. We laughed after Peter stopped swearing.'

'And then you found out who he was?'

'Yeah, he'd just robbed the bank down town. No wonder he was in a hurry.'

She became quite animated telling the story. It wasn't every day a bank robber got stuck in a dairy herd mid-getaway.

'They got him. He went up over the mountain and they got him in a road block. He couldn't have gone any other way. There's only one way out.'

I nodded. 'Was that the end of it?'

'No. The police came and thanked us for holding him up. Without us he would have got away. We held *him* up after he held the bank up,' she said and laughed at her little joke. 'Apparently they'd only just set up the road block when he came along. If he'd hit one of the cows properly he wouldn't have gone anywhere. Peter would have dealt with him.' She laughed a bit more.

'Do you usually have much trouble with the road crossing?' I asked.

'If people are too impatient to wait I just tell them to go steady and don't bump them. I go through first with my stick and try to make a path.'

'Are there many who won't wait?'

'Only you sometimes,' she laughed.

'What me? Impatient?' I replied, feigning surprise.

She was warming to this storytelling. And I'd thought she might have been hard to get going!

'You know, when you go real slow, the cows all want to stop and lick the car. If one does it they all want to. One bloke wanted me to stop them – told me his car was nearly brand new. What was I going to do? Jump up and hold all their mouths shut? Geez it was funny. He wound his window up real quick. He probably thought one might reach in the window and lick his face or bite his ear off or something. And then the cows wouldn't move at all because they'd found something different. Real curious they were. All tightly packed around his car. He didn't find it as funny as I did.'

'Have you ever seen him again?'

'Yes, but he waits back a bit till they've all gone across. I'm sure he thinks I don't recognise him.'

As we sat on the verandah talking, the milk tanker arrived to pick up thousands of litres of milk bound for the factory in Brisbane. The big semitrailer rolled quickly and confidently down the 50-metre lane – backwards – and pulled up precisely beside the door of the milk room.

'You've seen lots of changes Dolly – a far cry from the days of the old milk cans,' I prompt.

'Yes, and a good thing that. Remember the big old fridges? Dragging the cans in and out of them and up onto the truck? It was too hard, but we all did it. Give you a bad back.'

I nodded. I had only vague memories of the old 'can' days.

'Hello, Dianne,' Dolly greeted the tanker driver from the verandah. 'How's your mother? Back on top yet?'

'Yeah, Doll, she's right. Couldn't keep her down for long. How are you going?'

'Good. A bit tired. I stayed up half the night watching the tennis.'

'All night, every night isn't it?'

'Yeah. Better than most of that other rot.'

Dolly turned back to me, 'Did you know that Dianne's been driving the tankers for twenty-seven years?'

'Some sort of a record that'd have to be,' I answered, 'but not as big a record as yours, Dolly.'

She ignored my comment. 'Some thought it a bit of a joke when they gave her a go. You think back when she started. Not many girls were doing things like that.'

'Not many girls have worked nonstop like you have either, Dolly.'

She ignored that too.

'She's better than all the men. Never had an accident. She didn't even have a truck licence when they gave her a tryout over at the showgrounds.'

'Tell me about your garden, Dolly.'

Her 'garden' is a kilometre away from the farm, across the paddock and up the side of the range. It's not a garden as such – more a damp, rocky little self-contained rainforest.

'How do you know about that? Not many people do.'

'Oh, I've seen you walking up there,' I answered. 'Why don't you bring some of those orchids and staghorns down to the house, Dolly. They'd grow here.'

'They belong up there where they are, away from everything. That's their home in under the trees and the lantana. Don't ever tell anybody where they are or that will be the end of them.'

'I won't – now or ever,' I promised, feeling rather chastened.

'Anyway, I like to walk across the paddocks. It feels good, and I need the exercise.'

'It's a couple of kilometres there and back,' I say.

'That's not far.'

'Dolly, I saw you walking over to your garden early one morning last week and then saw you walking home from town a couple of hours later.'

'Yeah, Peter drove me down. He said he'd wait, but it was a nice day so I told him to go off wherever he was going.'

I wondered if Peter had ever considered running Dolly on the wing when he was playing A-grade football.

After a moment she said, 'Why don't you come down in the pit one morning? You haven't seen the new milking bails, have you?'

'No. I haven't. I should do that. I drive past a dozen dairies a day and never poke my nose into one.'

'It's pretty good. It takes about half the time to milk.'

'What about tomorrow morning?'

'All right. But when you come in, just speak quietly and no quick movements. Anyone or anything new and the cows all know. You watch – every single one will notice you.'

She stood up and turned towards the kitchen.

'Come down early. We're usually finished by seven. Now, do you want that cuppa?'

As I waited for the tea, I took in the scene before me. Green hills rolled to the forested foothills of the low range, its western slopes highlighted by the afternoon sun. It was only 3.30 in the afternoon, but the cows had already been turned out to the 'night' paddock. Their bellies full and their udders empty, one hundred and fifty sunlit backs swayed slowly away. Breaking the chain, one cow paused on the half-hearted pretext of having identified a tasty mouthful by the wayside. The next in line nearly ran into her rear end, then stood patiently, loath to step off the cattle pad. 'Hurry' has no translation in their language. An odd idea comes to mind. They are Holstein Friesians, maybe they understand German . . .

I've looked at this picture-postcard perfect scene a thousand times, but today I saw it as if for the first time.

Not long after daylight, I arrived for the morning milking. As I stepped into the new milk room I was startled by some cats who were equally startled by my arrival. Three abreast they competed to get through the doorway past me. In their haste to depart they upset their feed dish, lost traction in the spilt milk and converged in a tangle in the doorway, hissing their disapproval. Two started a skirmish on the run, but quickly reconsidered. After putting a safe distance between us they began to collect their wits, their arched backs and fizzed tails betraying their embarrassment. I don't think they were used to strangers at this hour of the morning . . . or ever.

The fresh paint and linseed putty of the new dairy gave off a pleasant aroma, but mixed with the smell of fresh milk and calf shit, their usual appeal was lost. I've always liked the smell of linseed and new paint, but this was faintly sickly.

Rivulets of frosty water coursed down the side of the circular cooling and storage vat that took up most of the room. Through the open lid I could see a couple of paddles rotating silently in a sea of milk.

It was cold in the milk room.

The wide sliding door to the herringbone bails was slightly ajar, so gingerly I put my head around the door jamb. Eight cows were being milked either side of the sunken pit in which the workers stood, their faces level with the cows' udders. In unison, every cow in every bail swivelled her head to examine me. They were inquisitive, not alarmed. Then, almost as one, they returned to the contents of their feed boxes.

'Come down into the pit here,' Dolly said.

She was looking after one half of the bails and kept her eyes everywhere.

'When I come to help, it relieves Peter so he can go and get the afternoon feeds ready.'

I nodded, then said, 'I know cows mostly kick sideways. Still it must be a bit unnerving with your head right down at their hoof level.'

'Not really. But if they try a backward kick, this bar here stops them. They only ever do that once or twice. It hurts their legs. More often they'll kick the cups off.'

She pulled the cups off one milker and attached them to the next cow.

'We've got a few new ones in this week. Some of them haven't learnt their manners yet.'

She'd barely uttered the words when one of them let fly with shit everywhere. 'It doesn't happen very often, only with the new ones. Some of them are a bit nervous,' Dolly said, stepping back smartly.

'You know, when I started milking, a real good cow would give three gallons a day. And a lot of others nowhere near that. Now some of these give 12 gallons and more. How many litres is that?'

I tried to calculate quickly. My metric wasn't much better than hers. 'A bloody lot, well over fifty.'

'Be a bugger to have to milk a herd of these by hand,' she said.

My attention was taken by one cow acting strangely. She was banging the top of her head on the feed chute. Dolly took no notice.

'What's she doing that for?' I asked her.

'She's as cunning as anything. Sometimes not all the feed drops down into the feed box and she's just checking. She's even figured out that if she keeps it up, half of the next cow's feed will slip down too if the baffle comes open just a bit.'

'Does she do it in every bail?' I look along and see that this is the only one, on this side anyway, that has a big dent in it.

'No, that's her bail. She comes to it every milking. They all come to their own bails.'

'True?'

She nodded. 'And they come into the bail in the same order all the time too. Some push in, others hang back and wait. It's the same every milking. Creatures of habit they are.'

'Do you know them all?' I ask.

'Mostly.'

'Surely not by name.'

'No, by number. It's on that plastic anklet they wear.'

'Milking cows all those years, Dolly —?' I was going to say more when she cut me off.

'Yeah, I like it.'

'For sixty-five years?' I finish my question.

'Sixty-five years here. Only came here when I got married. I started when I was eight years old in Dad's dairy. All hand milking then. Before I went to school and again when I came home. We all did it.'

'And if you don't mind me asking, how old are you now?'

'Eighty-eight now. Getting on a bit in years, but I still feel good. I suppose you've heard Peter's thinking of closing down. There's no money in it now. Pretty sad really after three generations.'

I followed her out to the calf pens. She wasn't wasting time standing about. We continued our conversation as she did her chores.

'So what will you do?' I asked.

'I might even retire properly now. Have to. I don't think anyone else would give me a job, do you?' she laughed, though I thought I detected a note of sadness too.

'You're a real gem, Dolly. Somebody might take you on – with a track record like yours they should.'

Typically she brushed my comment aside.

'No, I think I'll watch a bit more tennis. Might go and visit the girls now and then. Better if they come and visit me.'

Dolly and Peter had just finished feeding the calves when the seven o'clock news came on.

'We've finished right on time,' Dolly remarked.

'Seven o'clock finishing time, eh Dolly? Rain or shine, day in day out, year in year out?'

'Yeah. I'll probably still get up and come down here even if there are no cows. I'd look pretty silly, wouldn't I? Maybe after eighty years the only place I *can* listen to the morning news is in the dairy.'

SPEEDY PARR
Diesel and spinifex

———•◆•———

I'd read a paragraph about a bloke named Ian Parr in *Truck and Bus* magazine a while back. He sounded like a bit of a character and I was interested to find out more about him. A bush telegraph message helped me track him down – well, his mother anyway.

'He ran away from home when he was fifteen and we didn't know where he was for three years,' Dot Parr told me.

'Where'd he been?'

'On a property up in the Gulf country.'

This is the bloke for sure, I thought – elusive without trying to be, by default almost.

'It's a big country up there. Where'd you find him?'

'We didn't. He just materialised one morning, walked into the kitchen and said, "What's for breakfast?" I nearly had a heart attack. But it was so good to see him.'

Fleetingly she seemed lost to the present, reliving that moment. Then, as if her well-used mental picture was tucked away again, she said, 'I was just making a cup of tea. Would you like one?'

'Yes please. Just black will do nicely.'

While I waited for the tea I stood up and made my way around the photo gallery on her lounge room walls. If I'd done that in the first place, I'd have seen that my answers were all there. The room seemed to be divided into five sections – if you can imagine four walls being divided like that. Four batches of wedding photos and kids at various ages took up more than three-quarters of the room, and most of one wall was completely devoted to trucks – one hitched illegally with four semitrailers, others loaded with different kinds of freight, and an old blue Mack with three trailers loaded with dongas. In fact, there were lots of photos of an old blue Mack. And a single photo of a very young Ian, I guessed.

As Dot re-entered the lounge room I tried to remember where our conversation had left off.

She beat me to it. 'He's made his life up there. I call him our "Western gentleman". You know, one of his brothers is a solicitor, one an air traffic controller, another a teacher and so is his sister.'

'Is this the man in question?' I said, indicating the photo.

She nodded. 'Yes that's him, a long time ago.'

'Do you think they're all happier than he is?'

'No, I don't think any of the others are happier than he is. He's never happier than when he's working. And that's really all you want for your children, isn't it? But I wish he had someone to look after him.'

'Sounds like he's pretty good at looking after himself.'

'Yes', she said, 'it wouldn't be much of a life for a woman with him being away all the time like he is. Sometimes he lives in that truck for weeks at a stretch without getting home.'

'How long ago did he take off?'

'Forty years. He was employed on a property – Kamileroi, I think – at the start.'

'Where is he now?'

'Still up there – wherever his road train is. He has a depot in Cloncurry.'

'Can you give me a contact?'

'Yes; are you going to do a story about him?'

'If I can find him I might.'

'Call at the Post Office Hotel, they'll know where he is.'

Before I left, Dot took me on a guided tour of the photographic history around the lounge room. Good-looking couples with good-looking kids, Terry the fox terrier digging holes in the sand at Bribie Island, Dot's husband, Geoff, wearing his aircraft captain's uniform.

Cloncurry seems a long way from Brisbane because Cloncurry *is* a long way from Brisbane – about the same as Brisbane is from Cairns. It took me a week to get there: two or three days' solid travel and four or five days' holiday. I love that country. They say that if you ever cross the Diamantina you'll always come back – I've never heard of anyone who hasn't.

Dot Parr had been in contact with her son long before I sighted Cloncurry. When told of my mission his comment was, 'I'll be busy that day.' But he wasn't. Dot arranged for us to meet on the Saturday afternoon.

I knew to look for a dark-haired, straight-backed bloke about six foot tall, with a faraway look in his dark eyes. Dot Parr told me that he would probably be wearing a dusty, black, high-crowned ringer's hat. In that part of the country everybody's hat was dusty, so the only helpful part of that clue was the colour.

As I entered the bar I counted five dusty black hats – so that clue wasn't worth a cracker either.

Yet he *was* in the Post Office Hotel waiting for me – although, as things unfolded, I could have been forgiven for thinking otherwise. He didn't know who to look for, even though any stranger walking in right on time would have been a giveaway. I stood for a moment, listening to one of the black-hatted blokes at the tail end of a mobile phone conversation, and bought myself a light beer.

'Okay, mate. I'll be over in the morning to shift those little weaners. Shouldn't take long. I'll bring Mac and Kevin.'

He glanced towards me then got up. I looked expectantly towards him and thought he was going to come and extend a hand. Instead, with an almost imperceptible nod, he strode right past me to the toilet. I waited . . . and waited. Urgent call perhaps? Then I spotted him right down the other end of the bar talking quietly to an Aboriginal ringer. With his left hand on the back of a chair and his left arm straightened as if it was helping him stay upright, one boot crossed over the other with the toe planted firmly on the wooden floor, and a beer in his right hand, he looked like he was settling in.

He may not have realised who I was, or he may not have liked the look of me. I knew I'd have to risk it, so I went over.

'Er – Mr Parr? I'm Rhylle Winn, the bloke who's writing the book.'

'Yeah, I know. I've just got to fix Bob up here. Won't be long.'

'Have you got time to talk to me?'

'Yeah. What's the hurry?'

'Oh, no hurry.'

'Good.'

As he talked on for another minute or two, I retreated to my former position, not least to safeguard the money I'd left on the bar. A little apologetically I said to the barman, 'I needn't have worried. Suppose everybody's honest around here. Probably leave my money there all day, couldn't I?'

'Bullshit. It's a wonder it's still there now.'

I looked askance.

'No. It's not that bad. Some weekends it's not good though.'

'What, when the ringers all come to town?'

'No, not them. They're all good blokes. It's the bloody terrorists that cause the trouble. Ah, but there's some town buggers not too good either. You know, the ones that won't work.'

Ian came by at last, shook hands and drew up a stool.

'Just had to fix Bob up.'

I nodded. I was getting to know that Bob needed fixing up.

'He's got a start down south of here for the season. Chatsworth. They told him I used to work there, so he came over to see me for a bit of a knockdown. This interview business shouldn't take more than ten minutes, should it?'

'Well, by —' I was going to ask 'by whose clock', but stopped short, worried it might be taken the wrong way.

'If it's going to, then you'd better come with me,' he said, and without even waiting for a response he strode off once again, across the verandah this time, and gave an ear-drum splitting whistle that could be heard for a mile, maybe even a bit more. A tail-wagging, pink-eyed bull terrier emerged from the shade under the vehicle – an old ambulance with the windows and signage painted out. 'D9, get in here you old maggot bag!' he bellowed.

It crossed my mind that some bull terriers are deaf and that D9 might be one of them.

The dog licked his hand and bounded in – if bull terriers can be said to bound. Then Ian hopped in and drove off without looking back, leaving me standing there like a starched fart. I had assumed I'd be climbing in the passenger's seat beside him. I quickly tried to follow, but had locked my vehicle so that by the time I'd fiddled around and opened the door, the old ambulance had vanished around the corner. I tried to catch up, but it had disappeared into thin air.

Cloncurry isn't a big place, but you can still get lost in it. I know because I inspected the saleyards, Charlie Hudson's transport terminal, the new road to the Ernest Henry copper and gold mine and lots of other places. In fact, I was completely slewed.

Finally, I called into a shop – a little supermarket opposite a park – and asked if anyone knew where Ian Parr's transport depot was.

'I don't know. I only started last week,' the checkout girl answered in a lilting Irish accent. She might be a back-packer, I thought.

A bloke standing nearby said, 'Who?' And when I repeated the name Ian Parr, he said, 'Never heard of him, mate, and I've been here twenty-two years.'

What now?

'He drives a road train – a Ford LTL,' I added. It was a long shot, but I'd seen one amongst the photos on his mother's lounge room wall. It was the newest truck in his line-up, so I reasoned he might still be driving it.

'The only LTL in Cloncurry belongs to a bloke called Speedy. Hey, George, what's Speedy's other name?'

'Dunno. Ask Sylvia.'

'What's Speedy's other name?' he bellowed. No one turned a hair at the volume. They all must be used to it.

'She's deaf as a post, poor old bugger,' George volunteered.

I'd guessed that. But Sylvia and D9 both? Must be something in the water . . .

'Eh?' said Sylvia.

'For Christ's sake, what's Speedy's other name?'

'Parson, I think.'

That's close enough, I thought.

'Where's Speedy Parson's depot? Does anybody know?'

'Yeah, just around the corner here – a hundred yards down. I saw him come home only half an hour ago. Can't miss him. He drives an old ambulance.'

Well I'll be buggered.

I pulled into the depot and there was my new-found friend Speedy, lying on his back in a big patch of bindy-eyes, under the front of the ambulance.

'I got lost. Had a bugger of a job finding you.'

'Yeah, lose you blokes in a ten square mile horse paddock. Could have used you a bit sooner. Here, hop in the cab and put your foot on the brake pedal and hold it down till I tell you to let it out. Might have to do it a few times till I bleed them. I'll have to do both sides. Bugger of a job on your own.'

I obliged, shaking my head in disbelief because I didn't know what else to do – except look about. The LTL was parked outside a big shed so I'd got that right. The cottage was lowset and in need of paint. It had been in need of paint for many years. Only the steps were whitewashed – with sparrow shit from the nests above.

He slid out and said, 'Here, boy.' And wiped his hands on D9's back. The dog thought the attention was wonderful and I reasoned it must be pretty handy having a mobile hand cleaner following you about.

'Keeps the fleas off him. And keeps his stink down a bit. Bullies have an aroma all of their own. But this old boy only smells like diesel, or brake fluid or degreaser, don't you old mate?'

'How'd you come up with the name? Is it because he's such a big powerful bugger?'

He shook his head, 'D9 the K9,' he said deadpan, 'his father was V8.'

I thought he might enlighten me with another gem but he didn't.

'V8 the what?' I ventured.

'Just V8, because he was such a big powerful bugger,' he said, and nearly smiled.

'When I asked down at the store if they knew Ian Parr, everybody looked dumb. Nobody knew either your first name or your last. An old deaf lady told me she thought she'd heard of somebody called Speedy Parsons.'

'Yeah. Dumb buggers all right,' he said, pointing to 'Ian Parr Transport' embroidered above his pocket.

'What do they think that is? A pork chop? Who was there?'

'The checkout girl, a skinny bloke and another bloke – and then the deaf lady.'

He nodded.

'They probably think these shirts came out of the Vinnies bin. But I don't wear them much and I'm not here much.'

'How'd you get the name Speedy?'

'Tell you one day,' he said, 'if you behave.'

Mmm. Just as well I've got a week, I thought, but I didn't know how long Ian would want me about. Either way, it was no problem.

'Grab your swag,' he said as we headed upstairs. As we crossed the upstairs verandah he motioned towards a little room off to the left.

'In there okay by you?' Then he stopped, stepped back, and poked his head in around the doorway as if he'd never been in there before.

'Haven't seen him about for a while. He must have shed his skin and taken off.'

'Who must have?'

'Harry's left his calling card. He'll be back sometime.' Ian indicated a snake skin laid out artistically on the floor. I recognised the skin as that of a carpet python.

'Throw your gear in there. I don't get many visitors.'

'Only the second this year, eh?'

Nod.

Somewhat apprehensively, I did as I was told. In pride of place, slumped along the far wall, was a rusty old shearer's bed with the decaying wiring of one end drooping to the floor. There was nothing else in the room except for Harry's old skin. The door looked like it hadn't been shut for years – or ever.

'I don't expect you to put me up, Ian,' I said.

He looked at me as if he didn't know who Ian Parr was either.

'The name's Speedy. You wanted to have a talk. Didn't you? Well we can later.'

The kitchen was furnished in the same manner as my bedroom – sparsely. There was a table, one chair that looked solid and one that didn't, a fridge, stove and microwave.

'Have a seat. Want a beer?'

I was relieved to see it was light beer, so decided to break my golden rule. 'Thanks. Good idea.'

So this is a truckie's bachelor pad, I thought. The only adornment on the wall was a huge photo print of a prime mover hitched up to dozens of trailers. I was trying to count them as he closed the fridge door and saw me looking at it.

'Thirty-four,' he said as he handed me a stubby and screwed the lid off his. 'It's really something, isn't it?'

'Yeah, it's got me buggered,' I said, incredulous.

'The photo was taken at Winton at their festival,' Speedy explained. 'They put on a hell of a turnout every two years. Must take them two years to get over it – or they'd have one every year.'

'What's the story behind it?'

'It's a few years back now – probably about ten. The bloke there with the Toyota dealership always comes up with new ideas. They were trying to see how many trailers one prime mover could pull and how many would track around the corner before one mounted the footpath.'

'Christ, how would that have been on the clutch?'

'Ah, they've got a bog-cog. And there's just enough slack in each ringfeeder to have the strain come on to each one progressively – not all at once. Even so, I think they had a front-end loader giving it a shunt up the arse.'

'How many tracked around the corner?'

'About a dozen – count them. They track pretty good in the same line as the prime mover. The driver had pulled those trailers for two kilometres before he came to the corner.'

I was impressed.

'See what's pulling them?' he asked.

'Yeah, a bloody big prime mover.'

'A bloody big Ford LTL 9000 prime mover – same as that one,' he indicated through the window with a backwards jerk of his thumb, and beamed with pride.

I was more impressed.

'Hungry?' he asked.

'Yeah. Could eat the arse out of a low-flying duck.'

'Me too. You'll have to eat spag bol because there's nothing else.'

'Suits me.'

He hauled a huge pot from the fridge – which left it empty save for a half carton of beer. He ladled four great gluey dollops into a smaller container, replaced the pot and pushed the now-overflowing container into the microwave.

'Always make a pot of this stuff so it lasts a few days. I saved this bit when I knew you were coming.'

I was thinking of asking when he'd made it, but I didn't need to.

'Usually get sick of it by Friday, though, after a few days of nothing else.'

I calculated that this meant it was made on Wednesday at the latest and quite possibly any time before. Doubts crept in. But it was bloody beautiful – possibly the best I'd eaten. Must have been seasoned with something.

'It's good Ian – Speedy. You know your way around the kitchen.'

'Ah, tastes like shit, but it'll keep you alive.'

Later, we sat out on his little verandah and yarned about the beef industry, the drought, 12-ply Kumho tyres from Indonesia, the price of diesel, blue cattle dogs versus kelpies, ABC radio, Fords versus Kenworths, the weather, Slim Dusty and Lee Kernaghan and, to my astonishment, classical music. I was floored. I had no opinion on the last. I gathered that his CDs were his regular company. The word 'enigma' came to mind and stayed there.

'What made you run away from home when you were a kid, Speedy?'

'I didn't run away and I wasn't a kid – I was fifteen. I don't know what my old lady's told you.'

'Only that they couldn't find you.'

'I didn't run away. I took off. There's a difference. And I'd told everyone I was going to, so they shouldn't have been concerned. If I'd tried to do it any other way it wouldn't have happened.'

That seemed to be the end of it and, from his tone, I thought I might have overstepped the mark.

'No, I shouldn't have left them wondering for so long, but I never used to think about it. I was in a different world and it suited me fine.'

After a bit of a lull we decided to call it quits for the night. We were both surprised that it was ten o'clock.

'Well, Speedy, it's been a good yarn, mate.' I was somewhat disappointed that it hadn't lasted longer. I was sure there was so much more that he could tell me. 'I suppose you'll be gone before I'm up,' I said.

'What? You're coming aren't you? You're the one who wanted a story. Bloody long way to come for three minutes. See you in the morning,' he said and ambled off to bed.

God knows how long he'd been up before I surfaced.

'I heard rustling in the ceiling last night. Harry must be back, eh?'

'Yeah, he's home. Lucky he didn't come and claim his bedroom. He cleans up the rats and then has a sleep before he moves on. Does me a big favour.'

'What's on the agenda for the day, Ian?'

His eyes called me a fuckwit for using his Christian name again. 'Have something to eat first? You drink tea?' he asked as he slid a plastic jug into the microwave. 'Dunno what I'd do without this thing. We'll clean up the rest of that spaghetti for breakfast. Thank Christ that'll be the end of it. We won't be away long. Just a local job shifting some weaners. Don't have to leave just yet, but. I want to hose out the trailers and fit a new air filter first.'

I stood there, a little taken aback. My plans were quickly changing.

'I'd just assumed —' I started to say.

'Shouldn't ever assume anything mate, particularly in this country.'

'Okay. This *is* a surprise.' I was thrilled at the opportunity to continue.

With a slight smile he said, 'I just *assumed* you'd be coming. I told D9 he'd have to sit on the floor not the seat – and if there was any objection he could sit in the sleeper cab – and if he didn't like that he could go in the dog box – and if he didn't like that he could bloody stay home.'

'What'd *he* say?'

'Nothing – he's deaf.'

I should have seen *that* coming.

When Speedy didn't add anything further and didn't smile, I couldn't decide if he was joking or serious. I'd read stories of people who have animated discussions with their dogs. Maybe Speedy was one of them – although that quirky trait sort of belonged to the 'hatters' of the early backblocks; lonely shepherds and bound-ary riders.

He briefly eyed me, gauging my reaction. He must have known he had me in, but decided to let me down easy.

'He goes mostly on sight and vibration. Poor bugger'll get run over one day because of it. If there's a bit of traffic around and there's vibration from all directions he doesn't know where he is, poor sod.'

Speedy moved towards the shed to get a new filter and as the door swung open I could see an old blue Mack prime mover parked there with its front jacked up. He saw me focus on it and said, 'A pensioner this old relic. Still do a bit of light work with her, but – just local stuff.'

'Yeah, I recognise her.'

His brow furrowed. 'How? She's rarely been out of the shed for two years. You must be mistaken.' He didn't say any more and appeared happy to let the mystery be. Either that or he figured I'd say more sooner or later.

'There used to be a big white patch on the back of the cab. Last time I saw it there was,' I said.

'Well it's not there now. It's been gone for years. I'd cut some rust out before a respray. Shit you must have a good memory.'

'No, I saw it in a photo on your mother's lounge room wall less than a fortnight ago.'

'Still got a good memory. You know, the last job I did with the Mack was the best-paying job I ever had.'

'Yeah? What was it?' I thought I'd better say something in case he didn't continue.

'There was a message on my answering machine asking me to take a prime mover *only,* to Normanton – government job. "See the publican" it said. I tried to ring the agent back, but he'd gone to hospital or something so I decided to go to Normanton on spec. I couldn't think what the loading might be – must be something already on a trailer. Good jobs, government jobs – good money, and you get it within the month.'

'What was it?'

'The Mobile Breast Screen Clinic – to take back to the Curry. Top job that one.'

If you'd blinked you'd have missed the tiny smile.

He fitted the air filter, tidied up, and said, 'Throw your swag in the sleeper box.'

'What, are we staying overnight?'

He nodded.

'I thought you said there were only a few weaners to shift.'

I got another nod. That was it. *All in good time,* I thought.

'Hey Marge,' he called across the backyard to his next door neighbour, 'I've changed my mind about taking D9. Keep an eye on him will you? Won't be long.'

'Okay, but he'll put on a performance until you get to Middleton, or wherever you're going.'

'Yeah, let him off tonight, will you?' he asked, hooking the down-cast dog on the chain. 'Poor bugger, but he'd be a pain in the arse.'

It was midday before we got away, heading east. By that time the heat could kill a kangaroo and cook it.

'We'll pick up Kevin and Mac at McKinlay. Kevin will be there waiting. He's always on time. Mac's always late. If he's two hours' late he's an hour early. They've both got to come from Kynuna.'

'What are they coming for?'

'To help.'

Kevin wasn't waiting for us when we got there and I wasn't much help finding him. I didn't know who or what I was looking for. I couldn't keep firing questions, so I just watched and waited.

'Here comes Mac now. That's a bloody first!' Speedy remarked, after we'd waited about half an hour.

'What, where?'

Floating in from the east as if surfing the midday mirage a road train materialised. And the penny dropped. That made three bloody road trains with Kevin's. Christ!

'How many weaners are we shifting, Speedy?'

'They're only little – drought weaners pulled off their mothers early – about eleven hundred.'

I was struck dumb.

While we waited, Speedy suddenly became unusually animated.

'You know this was the pub they used in the film *Crocodile Dundee*,' he said proudly, 'Walkabout Hotel.'

'Yeah?'

He nodded. 'Some of us were extras and we were in the movie, but they edited us out. It was Mac's road train they used, you know, right at the beginning,' then as an afterthought, 'but for Christ's sake don't even mention it to him or we'll never hear the end of it.'

I was impressed.

'They're going to shift the pub out onto the main road so they can cash in on old Mick Dundee. They'll make a fortune.'

Presently Mac's rig rattled and bumped off the bitumen and hissed to a halt beside us.

'Where's Kevin?' Speedy asked.

'He's coming. This the writer bloke? G'day, mate, I don't think Speed can tell you much – he only says six words a day.'

If Speedy smiled I missed it.

'Where we going, Speed? Tooleybuc?'

Speedy nodded.

'That's what I thought you said. How many?'

'As many as you can fit on.'

'That's what I thought you said.'

'How big are they?'

'Christ, I don't know. They're half-starved weaners.'

'I think you did say that.'

'Shit, Mac, give us a break.'

'Okay, mate, don't get the shits.'

Speedy just sighed.

Kevin turned up an hour and a half later and neither Speedy nor Mac asked him why he was late. Perhaps because, to their way of thinking, he wasn't late. Finally we were under way; our own little convoy. After such an outpouring of words in the previous half-hour, Speedy seemed happy to trundle along in companionable silence.

The native fauna of the arid landscape barely acknowledged the road trains' intrusion. Close by the roadside, little companies of dusty red kangaroos lay prone, some scratching half-heartedly. They dozed in the thin shade of spindly saltbushes, whiling away the worst of the midday heat, completely still except for the occasional ear twitch. Plains turkeys stood rigid as we passed, blending so well with their surroundings that only the experienced eye could spot them until they moved. Here and there, kitehawks and wedge-tail eagles shadowed the rigs for short distances, trying to pinpoint any small lizard or rodent that might have been flushed out by the wind rush and vibration of the transports. Occasionally, white clouds of corellas filtered the sun, and rainbows of budgerigars flashed by.

Another road train loomed on the horizon – suspended like a hovercraft on a mythical lake. It prompted Speedy out of autopilot.

'Mick Curley. He just bought out Charlie Hudson's outfit.'

I waited for more – in vain. I wondered how the hell he could have identified the rig at that distance.

After Mick's rig thundered by, the radio crackled. 'Copy Speed. You got your handbrake on or are your fuel filters dirty? Ha ha ha!'

'Fuck off. At least I don't roll over all the time.'

'Don't get the shits, Speed.'

Click!

Poor bloody Speedy, I thought. He just tootles around quietly minding his own business and everybody thinks he's got the shits. Yet he just sits there looking about as worried as a cow with a bucktooth calf.

'Big country this, Speed.'

'Yeah, they're fucking it all up for us little blokes. Economies of scale.'

I was puzzled. 'Eh?'

'Yeah. Mick's got thirty-two rigs now, with Charlie's. Hard to compete.'

'I said "big country".'

'Oh, I thought you said "big company". Yeah. Gets in your blood. I think Dorothea Mackellar got it right.'

This bloke's no ordinary Aussie, I thought. He's a gem being cut slowly, every so often exposing another facet.

'Where are we actually taking these weaners, Speed?'

'Just around to Urandangie. They've had a bit of rain. This bloke's got a few stations here and there, and swaps cattle around a bit according to the seasons. Good for us blokes, good for the economy.'

'Exactly where is Urandangie?'

'Over on the Territory border.'

'Shit.'

'No, it's not far. Bugger of a track but. You wanted a story, didn't you?'

I nodded in reply, as he would have, and reminded myself of him. Talk about laid-back. At least I had a change of clothes in my swag. They lived there permanently as a pillow. We arrived at Tooleybuc with plenty of daylight left, but the decision was made to camp the night and load at first light.

Even though there was an invitation to stay in the guests' quarters, it sounded a little half-hearted and we opted to stay with the rigs and use the facilities in the ringers' quarters. We did accept the invitation for an early barbecue breakfast, though, and were very pleased we did.

'Hey, Speed. How many of these little buggers are there?'

'As many as you can jam in.'

'That's what I thought you said.'

'Shut up!'

'No need to get the shits, Speed.'

It took a couple of hours to load the weaners, and it went off like clockwork. Mac didn't have to jam them in, there was plenty of room.

'Bloody credit to these blokes to have this little mob of babies tailed out and educated like this. Somebody knows what they're doing,' Speedy said to me.

'That's what I thought,' came a voice from behind.

Speedy drew an audible breath.

The loaded rigs rumbled along slowly in procession, following the excuse for a road that ran parallel to the Hamilton River, down to the Boulia–Middleton Highway, then west.

'How far today, Speed?' I asked.

'Today and tonight till we get there. Straight through. Might stop somewhere for a feed. I've got the tucker box. How do you like the job?'

'It's an eye-opener. You blokes live in another world. I'm envious.'

'Yeah, Big Sky Country this – magnificent at night. I could never leave it. Not a day goes past . . .'

He trailed off.

I thought to myself, *Speedy will never go home to die – the Western Desert has claimed his heart. And anyway, he'd reckon it'd save on the freight costs.*

'This is min-min territory. Ever seen one?' I asked a little later.

He nodded.

I looked towards him questioningly.

'The blokes don't say much about them because if you do everybody thinks you're on the turps – or worse, the beans. Half the time they'd be right – but the other half, no. The bloody things would scare the Kumhos off a Kenworth.'

'I've seen one myself, just north of Birdsville at Cacoory bore. It wasn't bullshit either. There were seven of us in the camp and no booze,' I assured him.

'Haven't heard of them that far south before, but anything can happen in this country. I never take anything for granted.'

It was my turn to nod.

'How do you fellows get on with Mac?'

'Real good. Why? He's a top little bloke.'

'I thought he might get on your goat a bit.'

'No, why do you think that?'

'Always asks the same questions and he already knows the answers.'

'I hadn't noticed. One of the best blokes I've ever worked with,' he said, maybe even a little defensively.

Again, I was sorry I'd opened my mouth, but Speedy surprised me again when he continued speaking.

'Yeah, I had another good mate like him once. And it all got spoilt.'

He went quiet as if remembering some hurt. 'We'd both had too much rum. Makes sparrows fight emus, rum does. And we fought each other, outside the Blue Heeler Pub. Fought and fought, but neither of us could get the better of the other. They stopped it in the end. We'd battered each other half to death.'

'What was the argument about?'

'Same old story – neither of us could remember – or didn't want to remember.'

'Didn't you patch it up?'

'Yeah, we shook hands and went in and drank more rum.'

I didn't expect him to say anything further – but he did.

'It's never the same. Never is.'

He was still sorry. That was evident. I knew he'd get lost in his thoughts for a while then, so I did too.

The radio crackled with static. 'Hear me, Speed?'

'Yeah, Kev. What's up?'

'See those dirty black clouds out to the west?'

'Yeah.'

Click.

That was it. That was the whole bloody conversation.

'Nice bloke, Kevin, isn't he?'

'Yeah – never says much. He's like old D9 – reliable and he always comes when I call him.'

'I wonder how poor old D9's getting on, Speed.'

'He'll be right. Marge loves him. He'll be as fat as a pig when we get back and he'll be real sheepish because he'll know I know he's been sleeping on her bed.'

My mind crossed back to Speedy and reliable old Kev. With just the two of them it would be a fairly quiet camp. They'd need Mac there or it would be like a library. *Yeah, that's what I thought.* I made myself smile.

'How long have you and Kev worked together?'

'Years now – might be eight or ten.'

'Mac says Kev doesn't say more than half a dozen words in a day either. He told me last night that Kev was home for three days once before his missus realised.'

'Mac's full of bullshit. It was only two and a half. He was work-ing flat out at the depot, nearly round the clock, and only camped there because he thought his missus wasn't home.'

'Oh, so that's better is it? It's a wonder he didn't check.'

'Mightn't have thought of it. Might've forgot he had a missus.' Then he added, 'Bloody Mac says enough for both of us – three counting himself.'

'That's what I thought.'

Speedy glanced across at me. I nearly had him. He drew a breath and looked like he might be going to say something, or even smile, but he breathed out and did neither.

The big Ford ground to a halt and without a word Speedy slid out of the cab. I followed. Kev and Mac followed suit when they arrived – only a few minutes apart. There seemed to be a com-mon purpose, but I kept my mouth shut and waited. There had been no arrangement via the radios and I was a little mystified. After a brief three-way conversation that involved the words 'radi-als', 'Bridgestone', 'fuckin' useless bastard', 'low pressure', 'gauge fucked', 'compressor rooted', 'yeah fuckin' useless bastard all right', I gathered it was the state of their tyres and their tyre dealer they were discussing.

So my question was being answered without me having made a fool of myself. Then each man, armed with a solid short-handled lump hammer, progressed along his trailers. First he'd kick the outside tyre to make sure it still held air and then reach over and tap the inside dual to listen for the telltale hollow thud – or feel the hammer bounce to denote pressure.

Each rig was fitted with sixty-two tyres, and if too many were blown they'd be changed on the spot. Otherwise they could wait till they returned to the depot, I was informed.

As we proceeded, the tyre subject continued.

'Bugger of a job changing wheels on the road, eh Speed?'

'No, they're not so bad. You get used to that – plenty of practice. There're lots worse jobs.'

'Like what?'

'Once I had to replace an air line right under the cab – lying on my back, in bulldust about knee-high.'

'Yeah?'

'It was 47 degrees – a bloody scorcher.'

I nodded.

'Then it stormed. I didn't see it coming.'

'What happened?'

'I was stranded there for four days; lucky I was empty; but another time was worse.'

I waited.

'I had to get the big toolbox out, and after I'd finished the job I drove off and left it there and I was a kilometre or two down the track before I realised.'

How hard was it to go back? I thought.

'One of Mick's rigs rattled past before I could walk back, and covered it with a bloody great bow wave of bulldust. I had broken down in the middle of a bit of a flat. No trees or any landmark at all to get a bit of a fix on where I'd been – and I was only guessing how far I'd come.'

Bit of a flat – for Christ's sake it's all bloody flat, I thought, before I asked, 'Did you find it?'

'Yes, took me the best part of a day feeling around with my feet under the fairy floss.'

I shook my head.

'But that wasn't the worst bit. I knew I couldn't turn the rig around for at least 80 kilometres so I had to carry the box back.'

'Christ, what next.'

'It weighs 70 kilograms. Not that heavy – but bloody awkward. I suppose it could have been worse.'

I didn't say anything.

'It could have been both boxes. Usually I don't find everything I need in the first one.'

We were making good progress and were well past Boulia heading out through the ash downs country of Glenormiston on the Georgina River when we came upon an Aboriginal family sitting quietly in the shade on the roadside – in the middle of nowhere. They waved casually, half-heartedly even, as we bumped and rattled past.

'They didn't look too happy, Speed.'

'Yeah, they were right. They'll have somebody coming through tonight or tomorrow to pick them up. Patience is part of them. They don't get too excited about anything.'

'Neither would you if you'd just been covered in bulldust and half-choked – and with the prospect of the same happening a couple more times within the next few minutes.'

'No, they're right. If they'd wanted us for anything they would have stopped us. But it would have to be serious. They wouldn't bring a road train to a halt unless it was.'

'You get on well with them don't you.'

'They're just blokes and women like the rest of us, except they looked after Australia a lot better than we have – 40 000 years or more, probably a thousand generations, and you can't see where they've been, except for their brilliant art. A hard act to follow.'

The subject seemed closed and my mind turned to other things. Then, a little while later, Speedy continued – he'd obviously been thinking about his Aboriginal ringer mates. 'Their sense of humour really gets me. They get pleasure out of the simplest things. A toddler learning to walk can set the women off, or a rock thrown that startles a dog peeing up a bush can keep the kids amused for hours.'

'A simple life, eh?' I ventured.

'Yeah, some parts of it. But there's a lot you and I'll never know.'

I sensed a genuine respect.

'They're the best ringers this country will ever know. And a lot of the women are just as good as the men, if they don't get too fat. Same goes for the men to some degree.'

It was well into the night by the time we unloaded our weaners. They'd travelled well for youngsters, according to Mac.

'Where to now, Speed?'

'Nowhere yet. We'll stay here tonight.'

'That's what I thought.'

Speedy winked at me.

The same arrangements seemed to apply: token offer of the guests' quarters declined, musterers' quarters and barbecue breakfast accepted.

'Where to now, Speed?' I asked, waiting for a reaction.

'Don't you start. You haven't got any deadlines, have you?'

'No. Why?'

'Because the manager here took a call from Tobermorey last night and they've got a backloading of yearlings for the Cloncurry live export depot if we want it. It's a real stroke of luck. Make the job into a round trip, getting paid nearly all the way. Doesn't often happen.'

'Where's Tobermorey?'

'Back south a bit and just into the Territory.'

'Yeah, I'm interested.'

'That's good because we're going anyway.'

'How the hell would they know we were here?'

'Nothing goes on around this country without everybody knowing about it. It comes from looking after each other – cooperation bred into us. If you can't wear your identity on your sleeve you won't be blessed in the west.'

A little lesson at every turn.

The prospect of the Tobermorey backload put the transport owners in a good mood. Speedy was uncharacteristically jovial. So was Kevin. And Mac was dancing around trying to be funny – even more than usual.

'Shit, Mac, settle down a bit. You're like a blowfly in a pickle bottle,' Speedy jibed, but the observation had no effect on Mac.

However there were other, practical, considerations.

'A good, profitable cheque can disappear into thin air in that country,' Speedy told me, 'eaten up in tyre replacements, and the other blokes know it only too well.'

The road down to Tobermorey was through flinty country. I'd not heard the term before, but it sort of explained itself.

'Murderous on tyres at different times.'

'Why not all the time?'

'Because when they put the grader over it, the blade stands the little flints upright. Makes a good road when they're all flattened out. But it's better to be in front of the grader than behind it.

'So at least we know to keep plenty of air in the tyres – stand the walls up straight. You wouldn't think those little stones could pierce heavy truck tyres, but they do, especially with a load on when the tyres sag a bit – chops the walls out of them.'

As we set off, the three drivers' light-hearted jauntiness seemed to extend to their rigs. The damaged tyres had been replaced and, now running empty, the transports responded easily to the throttle. As we settled into the trip, the fine weather and the prospect of good profits had put Speedy in a talkative mood – as talkative as he gets anyway.

'Speed, what's the worst trip you've ever had?'

'I'd been down to Bourke with a load of brumbies. From Normanton to Bourke – the full length of Queensland, and then some more – they'd been bastards to load and bastards to travel. Shit they were a poor lot – inbred, run-out, Roman-nosed mongrels. But it wasn't them that caused the trouble.'

'Why to Bourke?' I kept on.

'It's got the only abattoir accredited to slaughter horses for human consumption for export to Europe.'

'Turns the guts a bit – eating horse meat.'

'Yeah, but those Continental carnivores would eat anything. They slaughter wild goats, donkeys, camels, pigs – wild boar they call it. Slaughter them all at Bourke.'

'So what did cause the trouble?'

'It was the backload of skinny bullocks,' he said as he slowed the heavy transport and moved onto the shoulder to let another rig pass. 'They had to go Windorah in the Channel country for fattening. I was working for Charlie then. I'd have preferred to go straight home empty because it was just before the wet – but Charlie was the boss.'

'Sounds pretty harmless so far,' I ventured.

'Would have been, too. The timing was right enough, except that there was a false start to the wet. I was marooned for three weeks – bogged to the axles, *really* bogged.'

'Three weeks!'

He nodded. For a while it seemed that was the end of the story. He was pretty good at understatement.

He nodded, then knocked back three gears in quick succession as the rig laboured slightly at one of his so-called 'jump-ups'. I had a vision of a jump-up being a steep escarpment, but it was more of a low hill. I'd not even seen this one looming. For a while

I thought he'd forgotten to finish his story. He was pretty good at saving words.

'Yeah, as luck would have it I was on a bit of higher country and as it kept raining it became an island.'

I knew about his higher country now – imperceptible to the eye of coastal folk I bet. 'What about the bullocks?'

'I had to jump them off after a couple of days – not that easy with trailers bogged more on one side and all tilted over.'

An image came to mind of trailers toppling over in the mud and terrified cattle scrambling to get free. A second image, a split second later, had the cattle on the bottom deck completely trapped. A ghastly thought.

'Were any damaged?'

'Yeah, a few. They broke their legs as they jumped off. It shouldn't have happened, and I couldn't see why it did.'

'What could have caused it?'

'Nothing that I could figure, but I'd heard of brittle bone in some cattle that come off calcium- and phosphorus-deficient country and wondered if it could have been that. I never found out for sure.'

'Were the cattle all stranded on the island with you then?'

'No, I hunted them all off before it closed over.'

'The damaged ones too?'

'Yeah, I had to. The last thing I wanted was to have to share the place with half a dozen crazed bullocks.'

He read my thoughts. 'They heal up pretty good you know. Lots of bullocks have a bit of a limp. But I suppose you never get to see the ones that don't recover. I had plenty of other company without them.'

I looked over at him questioningly.

'A roo, a dingo pup, dozens of lizards, one big old sand goanna, and bloody snakes everywhere. I don't know if I kept seeing the same ones over and over, but there seemed to be dozens. Anyway, it was overcrowded with just one of the buggers. I had to keep the cab door shut so at least I could sleep in safety. Did you know that the western taipan is the deadliest snake on earth?'

'I knew it was in the top ten. Did you kill the snakes?'

'At the top of the top ten mate. And yeah, when I could.'

'What about tucker?'

'That big sand goanna kept a good eye on me. The Murris love them – one of their favourite dishes.'

'Why didn't you have a go at him?'

'Because I had no wood for a fire – otherwise I would have.'

'Did you have plenty of other tucker?'

'Always keep a full tucker box, but it wasn't too good because, like I said, I had no wood for a fire and had to eat most of it cold – nearly a full carton of tinned baked beans and half a one of spaghetti. I kept the spaghetti till last because I like it better than beans.'

I took that in, imagining the diet.

'After about ten days, I could struggle about enough to gather a bit of wood. When that old goanna saw me come back with the first armful he scuttled off and dived into the water, paddling like hell and looking back over his shoulder.'

It was the first time I'd heard Speedy actually laugh out loud.

'Would have been bloody boring by the end, wouldn't it?'

'No. I kept myself busy. Always like to be doing something.'

I thought he was having a go at me.

'Like what?'

'Killing bloody sandflies – millions of them. Big bastards and hungry too. No, I had a book, *Lonesome Dove*. Read it three times. Kept finding bits I must have skipped over the time before. Have you read it? It's a good yarn. I'll give it to you later.'

American Westerns weren't exactly my choice of reading material, but I tried to look pleased about the prospect.

Both the loading at Tobermorey and the trip back to Cloncurry were uneventful. Despite Speedy's concerns, tyre damage hadn't been a problem. For me the whole trip was exciting. I hadn't been able to believe my good fortune at having the opportunity. But by the end I was dirty and tired.

D9 was pleased to see us back, to see Speedy back anyway. He wasn't any fatter and I didn't think he looked sheepish – bull terriers' faces aren't particularly expressive – but Speedy thought he did. As I was packing my bit of gear, Speedy came over and handed me *Lonesome Dove*. I wasn't getting away without it. It was the most tattered, dog-eared volume I'd ever seen. In fact, it was nearly two books – only a flimsy stretch of binding still holding the two halves together. There were plenty of loose pages, dozens out of a total of a whopping eight-hundred or so.

'We'll have a yarn about it the next time I see you,' he said.

'Wonder when that'll be?'

'Never know. This country is full of surprises.'

'Well, if you're down Brisbane way – if you ever do come back home – give us a call. You'll be welcome to stay.'

'Home isn't Brisbane mate. I left it forty years ago because I didn't like it.'

Just then his phone rang. By the conversation I could tell it was another job.

'Yeah, mate – Mt Isa saleyards down to Hughenden. Yeah, just back – little round trip, backload from Tobermorey. Yeah. Six o'clock. I'll fill the tucker box on the way.'

'Six o'clock. Do you mean straight away?'

'No, I'll have a shower first.'

'When do you ever have a spell?'

'Never when there's work about. Enough time off during the wet.'

'You love it up here, don't you?'

'I'm part of it, or it's part of me. I could never leave it now.'

With that he went inside. I was still there when he came out – about five minutes later.

'I'll send you a copy of the book when it's published.'

'No, send it to my mother. I've got the rest of my life to read it. Anyway I don't want any of these buggers up here reading it. You'll probably put a lot of bullshit in it.'

'If I call you Ian Parsons, nobody will know who it's about.'

'Nuh. I'll see it when I go down to see the oldies at Christmas.'

There was a finality about that statement. His inscrutable far-away look had returned. We shook hands and that was it. 'Come on D9. Let's go,' and the truckie and his very happy dog beat me out of town.

I called on Dot Parr when I returned home, to say thanks, and to tell her that her Western Gentleman was alive and well.

'Oh you found him. That's good.'

'He told me that he would be down to see you at Christmas.'

'Did he mention which year?'

I smiled and so did she.

Acknowledgements

There are nine characters in this book and I'd like to thank eight of them who graciously cooperated with my intrusion into their lives: Kylie Briais, Ian Parr, Rob Hughes, Ray Dahl, Mrs Dolly Leis, Leigh Henzell, George Wilson and Oscar Neilson (may he rest in peace). I left the ninth out, ever so modestly, because it is me.

Thanks also to Olive Quilty, for permission to quote from Tom Quilty's *The Drover's Cook*.

I would also like to thank publisher Ali Watts and editor Miriam Cannell for their professional work and for making this project so rewarding and so much fun. I hope this is just the beginning.

Wild Ride

The Rise and Fall of Cobb & Co

SAM EVERINGHAM

In 1853, a young American arrived in the new colony of Victoria hoping to make his fortune from the world's richest gold rush. He soon realised that the real money was to be made from the miners' needs to travel from the fields where they found their gold to the towns where they spent it, and established a coach company that would literally carry his name into every household in the land: Cobb & Co.

But Freeman Cobb himself was long gone by the time the company bearing his name became an Australian legend. *Wild Ride* is the story of two extraordinary men, James Rutherford and Frank Whitney, who transformed Cobb's humble company into the Qantas of its day, dominating transport and communications from Castlemaine to Cooktown and owning much of the land in between. These were pioneers, carving a path through otherwise impassable terrain, enduring attacks by bushrangers and terrible accidents, and making their fortunes. The Rutherford and Whitney families became two of the most significant of their era, unrivalled in their influence and, finally, vicious in their falling out.

Written with unprecedented access to the families' letters and diaries, *Wild Ride* reveals the Cobb & Co story in all its drama, conflict and tragedy. It is the compelling story of Australia's first great company and the people who made it.

Subscribe to receive *read more*, your monthly newsletter from Penguin Australia. As a *read more* subscriber you'll receive sneak peeks of new books, be kept up to date with what's hot, have the opportunity to meet your favourite authors, download reading guides for your book club, receive special offers, be in the running to win exclusive subscriber-only prizes, plus much more.

Visit penguin.com.au to subscribe.